Anonymus

North western Ontario

Its boundaries, resources and communications

Anonymus

North western Ontario
Its boundaries, resources and communications

ISBN/EAN: 9783742876331

Manufactured in Europe, USA, Canada, Australia, Japa

Cover: Foto ©Andreas Hilbeck / pixelio.de

Manufactured and distributed by brebook publishing software (www.brebook.com)

Anonymus

North western Ontario

ITS

BOUNDARIES, RESOURCES

AND

COMMUNICATIONS.

*PREPARED UNDER INSTRUCTIONS FROM THE
ONTARIO GOVERNMENT.*

Toronto :
PRINTED BY HUNTER, ROSE & CO., 25 WELLINGTON STREET WEST
1879.

TABLE OF CONTENTS.

	PAGE.
NORTH-WESTERN ONTARIO	1
Boundaries	1-2
Area	2-3
Population	3
Lakes and Rivers	3-4
Agricultural Capacity	4

ERRATA.

On page 2, line 1st, for " south " of the said river read " source " of the said river.
On page 3, fourth line from foot, for Rainy " River " read Rainy " Lake "
On page 7, under head " Inducements to Settlement," second line, for " southern " read " western."
On page 27, first line, for " York " read " Nelson," and on sixth line, for " western " read " eastern."
On page 40, fourteenth line from top, for " most " read " more."
On page 63, sixteenth line from foot, for " north-east " read " north-west."

Progress in Civilization	18
Numbers included in Treaty No. 3	18
Geological Features	18-21
Lac des Mille Lacs to Winnipeg River	21-23
Line of the Canadian Pacific	23
Climate	23-26
EASTERN DIVISION :	
Lake Superior to James Bay	26-7
Routes to Hudson's Bay	27-8
Lake Huron to Moose Factory	28-9
Moose Factory to Michipicoton	29-30
Black River to the Albany	31-4
Lake Nepigon to Albany	34-7
Lake Abbitibbe Route	37-8
Lake Nepigon to Lake St. Joseph	38-9

TABLE OF CONTENTS.

	PAGE.
NORTH-WESTERN ONTARIO	1
Boundaries	1-2
Area	2-3
Population	3
Lakes and Rivers	3-4
Agricultural Capacity	4

WESTERN DIVISION :

Lake Superior to Lake of the Woods	4
The Dawson Route	5-6
Canadian Pacific Railway	6
Improvements of the Lake Route	6-7
Inducements to Settlement	7
Kaministiquia Valley	7-8
Valley of the Matawin	8-9
Height of Land	9
A Pine Region	9
Rainy River	10-11
Supply of Pine Timber	11-12
Alberton	12-13
Adjacent Territory in Minnesota	13-14
Fort Frances Lock	14
The Indians	14
Number Three Treaty	14-16
Terms of the Treaty	16-17
Subsidies and Presents	17-18
Progress in Civilization	18
Numbers included in Treaty No. 3	18
Geological Features	18-21
Lac des Mille Lacs to Winnipeg River	21-23
Line of the Canadian Pacific	23
Climate	23-26

EASTERN DIVISION :

Lake Superior to James Bay	26-7
Routes to Hudson's Bay	27-8
Lake Huron to Moose Factory	28-9
Moose Factory to Michipicoton	29-30
Black River to the Albany	31-4
Lake Nepigon to Albany	34-7
Lake Abbitibbe Route	37-8
Lake Nepigon to Lake St. Joseph	38-9

	PAGE.
Physical Peculiarities and Aspect	39-41
James Bay	41-2
Moose Factory	42-4
Climate at Moose and Albany	44-5
Mineral Resources of James Bay and Neighbourhood	45-8
Wild Animals of North-Western Ontario	48-50
Indians of James Bay	50-1
HUDSON'S BAY	51-2
Nelson River Valley Route	52-4
Climate	54-7
Soil and Climate at York and Churchhill	57-9
Navigation of Hudson's Bay	60-1
Hudson's Straits	61-3
Fisheries, Minerals, and Commerce	63-4

NORTH WESTERN ONTARIO,

ITS

Boundaries, Resources and Communications.

By the award of the Arbitrators, to whom was referred the duty of determining the Northern and Western Boundaries of the Province of Ontario,* a vast and magnificent territory has been declared to be within the jurisdiction of the Ontario Government and Legislature. This fine region contains within its limits, timber lands of great value, rich and varied mineral deposits, rivers and lakes of noble proportions,—abounding in fish, and opening up remote districts to travel and commerce,—and touches at once the head waters of the St. Lawrence navigation and the shores of a great northern sea, the treasures of which, when sought with the ardour and appliances of modern enterprise, may yield a return not even dreamed of by those old explorers and navigators who were most sanguine of its resources. The possession of such a country necessarily entails upon its rulers some burdens and many responsibilities. To preserve peace and order, to administer justice, to maintain civil rights, to encourage settlement, to improve existing means of communication, to promote education, are duties coming, under the law, within the functions of Provincial authority. It is therefore important to ascertain the advantages likely to accrue to the people of Ontario from the assumption of the new or additional obligations incidental to the possession of this extensive domain.

THE BOUNDARIES.

The question of boundary set at rest by the award, had been the subject of much laborious investigation.† • The Dominion Government contended that the northern boundary of Ontario was the height of land forming the watershed of the St. Lawrence and great lakes, and skirting, at distances varying from fifteen to fifty miles, the northern shores of Lakes Superior and Nepigon. The western boundary, it was contended, was to be ascertained by a line drawn due north

---

* Con. Statutes (Ont.) cap. iv. The Arbitrators were, Chief Justice Harrison, Sir Francis Hincks, and Sir Edward Thornton, the British Minister at Washington.

† See Report on the Boundaries of Ontario, by David Mills, 1873; also an Investigation of the Unsettled Boundaries of Ontario, by Charles Lindsey, 1873.

from the confluence of the Ohio and Mississippi Rivers, and which was found to be in longitude 89 deg. 9 m. 27 sec. west. Such a line would have intersected Thunder Bay, divided the existing settlements on its shores, alienated from Ontario a large district—including the Village of Prince Arthur's Landing, the population gathering round Fort William, the site of the projected terminus of the Canadian Pacific Railway, and the Townships of Blake, Crooks, Pardee, Paiponge, Oliver, Neebing, and McIntyre, already under Ontario jurisdiction,—and left within the Province, only a narrow strip north of the lakes and south of the height of land. Opinions were divided as to the rights of the Province beyond the boundaries contended for in behalf of the Dominion, but it will probably be found that the decision of the arbitrators is, on the whole consistent with equity, convenience, and public policy. The award declares that the following are and shall be the boundaries of the Province of Ontario, namely :—" Commencing at a point on the southern shore of Hudson's Bay, commonly called James Bay, where a line produced due north from the head of Lake Temiscamingue would strike the said south shore, thence along the said south shore westerly to the mouth of the Albany River, thence up the middle of the said Albany River and of the lakes thereon to the south of the said river at the head of Lake St. Joseph, thence by the nearest line to the easterly end of Lac Seul, being the head waters of the English River, thence westerly through the middle of Lac Seul and the said English River to a point where the same will be intersected by a true meridional line drawn northerly from the international monument placed to mark the most north-westerly angle of the Lake of the Woods by the recent Boundary Commission, and thence due south following the said meridional line to the said international monument, thence southerly and easterly following upon the international boundary line between the British possessions and the United States of America into Lake Superior. But, if a true meridional line drawn northerly from the said international boundary at the said most north-westerly angle of the Lake of the Woods shall be found to pass to the west of where the English River empties into the Winnipeg River, then and in such case the northerly boundary of Ontario shall continue down the middle of the said English River to where the same empties into the Winnipeg River, and shall continue thence in a line drawn due west from the confluence of the said English River with the said Winnipeg River until the same will intersect the meridian above described, and thence due south following the said meridional line to the said international monument, thence southerly and easterly following upon the international boundary line between the British possessions and the United States of America into Lake Superior."

AREA.

The district included within these boundaries is of equal if not of greater area than the whole of the rest of Ontario, exclusive of the Lakes Ontario, Superior, Huron, and Erie. Omitting those lakes, the Province, within the limits embraced in the proposition of the Dominion, contained about 64,000,000 acres, or 100,000 square miles of territory. From the Quebec boundary line—from Lake Temiscamingue to James Bay—to the Lake of the Woods, the distance cannot be much less than seven hundred miles; while, measured from north to south, the new territory covers a breadth of country varying from over three hundred to one hundred miles. The Province of Ontario will consequently, in future, possess an area of fully 200,000 square miles. This is 80,000 square miles greater than the area of the United Kingdom; only 12,000 square miles less than the whole German Empire; only 2,000 square miles less than France; and equal to the combined areas of Holland, Portugal, United Italy, Switzerland and Belgium. The awarded territory, alone, possesses an area greater by 20,000 square miles than the group of countries just named, excepting Italy.*

POPULATION.

The present population of the territory is chiefly confined to the settlements on the north or north-west shore of Lake Superior, and in the valley of the Kaministiquia, to the colony at Fort Frances, on Rainy River, to a few settlers and Hudson's Bay officials at Moose and Albany on James Bay, and to the Indians, who are to be found mostly at Rainy River, the Lake of the Woods, Lac Seul, and Pigeon River. A few Half-breeds and christianized Indians are also settled at Islington, on the Winnipeg River, and around some of the Hudson's Bay Company's factories. The total population, including, of course, the Thunder Bay settlements, is probably under 10,000, half of whom are Indians and Half-breeds.

LAKES AND RIVERS.

In the more southerly portion of the territory lies the chain of rivers and lakes forming what has been popularly known as the Dawson Route, from Thunder Bay to Fort Garry. The western central portion is intersected by the Canadian Pacific Railway from Fort William to Rat Portage. The principal rivers of the territory are:—The Albany, flowing north-eastward to James Bay from Lake St. Joseph, which lies on the northern boundary line, about midway between the Bay and Winnipeg River; English River, which, leaving Lac Seul, after throwing off a branch to the southward, finds its way to the Winnipeg; the Seine, a fine stream, that, coming from the north-east, is finally lost in Rainy Lake; the Manitou, flowing due south from the lake of that name to Rainy River; the Kaministiquia and its confluent the Matawin, falling into Thunder Bay; the Moose River, emptying itself into James' Bay, and which divides into three large branches, known as the Missinibi, flowing northward from Lake Missinibi, just

---

* Mr. Devine, Deputy Surveyor-General of Ontario, gives 97,000 square miles as a rough approximate estimate of the area of the awarded territory. Other authorities, however, consider 120 to 140,000 sq. miles to be its probable extent.

north of the height of land that divides that lake from the head waters of the Michipicoton River; the Mattagami, or South Branch of the Moose; and the Abbitibbe, which runs from Lake Abbitibbe, lying upon but chiefly to the westward of the Quebec and Ontario Boundary line,—until it joins the main stream to the south of Moose Factory. Should the difficulties attending the passage of Hudson's Straits prove to be a more serious hindrance to their navigation than modern appliances can successfully overcome, the tendency would be to give to Ontario the benefit of any traffic that might be generated in Hudson's Bay, or on its coasts, and which would seek an outlet by way of the Moose or Albany Rivers, or by other means of communication with the great lakes.

Agricultural Capacity.

The value of the territory in an agricultural sense, will have to be largely determined by the facilities afforded for the development of other industries. Should its fisheries, its forests, and its mines yield a return at all proportionate to present indications, the agriculturist will find an ample demand for the produce of large sections of country which will well repay cultivation. In noticing the features and resources of the territory more in detail, it will be most convenient roughly to divide it into two sections, one that may be generally described as lying between Lake Superior and Lake of the Woods, the other between Lake Superior and James Bay.

WESTERN DIVISION.

Lake Superior to Lake of the Woods.

From Fort William, at Thunder Bay, to the Lake of the Woods, according to the course taken by the Canadian Pacific Railway, which crosses the waters of the latter at Rat Portage, its northern extremity, the distance is 298 miles.* The Dawson route, which, following the navigable waters, curves to the southward until it reaches the International Boundary line, which it follows until the North-west Angle is reached—involves a journey of 357 miles.† The latter may in fact be described as the arc of a circle of which the railway-line is the chord. South of the railway, and connecting it at various points with the water route, are innumerable lakes and streams, some navigable for large boats, others with occasional portages, for canoes, so that it has been said an Indian in his canoe may traverse the whole region with little impediment or difficulty.

---

* Report Canadian Pacific Railway, 1877.
† Report Public Works. Sess. papers (Canada), 1875.

The Dawson Route.

The Dawson Route was originally designed to form a means of communication through Canadian territory with the Red River Settlements. The partial construction, however, of the Canadian Pacific Railway, and the completion of railway communication between Duluth and Red River, have supplanted the older route, which must henceforth be regarded mainly in connection with local colonization and industries. To this object the fine road from Thunder Bay to Lake Shebandowan, the Fort Frances Lock on Rainy River, and numerous improvements on the intermediate waters and portages may all be made largely subservient. A brief description of the route itself will give a very fair idea of the peculiar characteristics of the region it traverses.* From Thunder Bay to Lake Shebandowan by road, the distance is 45 miles. The remainder of the route is represented as follows :—

	Miles.	Miles.
Lake Shebandowan		18·00
Portage	0·75	
Lake Kashebowie		9·00
Height of Land Portage	1·00	
Lac des Mille Lacs		18·50
Baril Portage	0·25	
Lake Baril		8·00
Brulé Portage	0·25	
Lake Windegoostegan		12·00
French Portage	1·75	
Lake Kaogassikok		15·00
Pine Portage	0·38	
Lac deux Rivieres		1·22
Deux Rivieres Portage	0·40	
Lake Sturgeon		16·00
Maligne Portage (lift)		
River Maligne		10·00
Island Portage	0·06	
Lake Nequaquon		17·00
Nequaquon Portage	3·25	
Lake Nameukan		15·00
Kettle Falls Portage	0·12	
Rainy Lake		44·00
Fort Frances Portage (now avoided by the Lock)	0·12	
Rainy River and Lake of the Woods, to North-west Angle		120·00
	8·33	303·72
To Rat Portage is 35 miles further		

We shall notice presently the method by which it is suggested the necessity for transhipment at the portages may be overcome, and a journey along the whole route be performed with comparative ease. Meantime, it is worthy of notice that the settlers along a line of country, over 300 miles in extent, may secure com-

---

* Report Public Works. Sess. papers (Canada), 1875.

munication by the cheap and ready means afforded by a series of splendid water stretches, varying from one to one hundred and twenty miles in length, and interrupted by only eleven portages, eight of which are less than a mile, and two under two miles, while only one exceeds three miles in length. The facilities for communication are not, however, actually confined to the waters on the line of the Dawson Route. South of the Thunder Bay and Shebandowan Road, are the Kaministiquia and Matawin Rivers, both fine and navigable streams, and, along the International Boundary line, are Pigeon River, Lake Sageniga and Basswood Lake, connected with Nequaquon Lake, already mentioned as a link in the chain of the Dawson Route. From the north-east, navigable by boats for 30 miles from its mouth, and for over 100 miles for the passage of timber, the Seine empties itself into Rainy Lake at Sturgeon Falls, while the Manitou—also a fine river—approaches the same lake from a more northerly source.

THE CANADIAN PACIFIC RAILWAY.

The Canadian Pacific Railway has, meantime, become a most important factor in connection with the colonization of the region under consideration. It was originally intended that the line, after leaving Fort William, should deflect to the southward, in order to touch the water route at Sturgeon Falls at the head of a navigable arm of Rainy Lake. By the construction of the Lock at Fort Frances and the removal of a few obstructions in the Rainy River, an unbroken line of some 200 miles of regular communication would have been established between Sturgeon Falls and the crossing of the Lake of the Woods, at any spot determined upon whence another section of the railway would have been constructed to Red River But, for engineering reasons, the railway has been carried farther north, and now first touches the navigable waters at Port Savanne, situated at the northern extremity of Lac des Mille Lacs, 71 miles from Thunder Bay.

IMPROVEMENTS OF THE LAKE ROUTE.

The best mode by which traffic may be maintained between Lac des Mille Lacs and Lake of the Woods, has been the subject of investigation before a Committee of the House of Commons.* At Lac des Mille Lacs, the height of land is reached separating the waters that flow into Lake of the Woods from those that find their outlet in Lake Superior. From Port Savanne to the head of Rainy Lake, the distance is about 112 miles, with $6\frac{1}{2}$ miles of portaging. Adopting the suggestions of Mr. Hugh Sutherland, Superintendent of Public Works in the Northwest, the Commons Committee, in their report, advised the construction of tramways upon the portages between Port Savanne and Kettle Falls, to be worked with light narrow-guage cars drawn by horses, the cars being run on the barges,

---

* Report Select Standing Committee on Immigration and Colonization, House of Commons, 1878.

and thus transferred with their freight, without breaking bulk or requiring transshipment. Mr. Sutherland was of opinion that these works could be executed for a sum of $150,000 in one season, and "that they would lead to the colonization of cultivable tracts along Rainy River, and other ports of the Dawson Route, and also furnish the Province of Manitoba with increased facilities for obtaining lumber at a much cheaper rate than at present." What this would do for the lumberers of Ontario will be noticed further on. To complete the information respecting the accessibility of this portion of the territory it is only needful to add, that the Canadian Pacific Railway is being rapidly completed to English River, 113 miles west from Thunder Bay, and that the link between Rat Portage and Selkirk on Red River, 23 miles north of Winnipeg, with which it is connected by railway, is also under construction. The country lying directly west of the North-west Angle of the Lake of the Woods was long since rendered accessible by a good road from the Angle to Fort Garry.

INDUCEMENTS TO SETTLEMENT.

Having noticed the means of access to, and internal communications of the southern portions of the territory it becomes necessary to consider what attractions it may possess in itself to the settler or speculator. The exhaustive explorations of Canadian Pacific surveyors and their associates have done most towards affording information on this head.

KAMINISTIQUIA VALLEY.

Professor Macoun,* in his report to the Dominion Government, after repelling the current opinion that the western shores of Lake Superior are unfit for settlement on account of the severity of the climate, and remarking that "the vegetation around Lake Superior is noted for its luxuriance," thus describes the aspect of the country in the vicinity of the Kaministiquia:—"As the traveller proceeds up the river, roses (*Rosa blanda*) begin to appear. By the time two miles are passed, black-ash (*Fraxinus sambucifolia*) shows on the banks, and the undergrowth becomes almost identical with that of the rear of Hastings and Frontenac, on the shore of Lake Ontario. A few miles further, and forms peculiar to a dry soil begin to take the place of those seen further down, while the alluvial flats along the river support a most luxuriant growth of just such plants as would be seen on any river bottom in Eastern or Central Canada. Thickets of wild plums (*Prunus Americana*), three or four different cherries, gooseberries, currants, raspberries and strawberries grow in profusion, interspersed with various species of Viburnum and other caprifolaceous plants. The herbaceous ones were very numerous and luxuriant, and these, including the wild pea (*Lathyrus venosus et ochrocolencus*), and the vetch (*Vicia Americana*), caused such tangled thickets that it was almost an impossibility to force our way through them. Wild hops (*Humulus Sapulus*),

---

* Appendix C to Report Canadian Pacific Railway, 1874.

climbed up almost every tree. For the whole distance up to Kakabeka Falls there was a constant influx of new species having a westward tendency. Between Kakabeka Falls and the mouth of the river I detected 315 species, all of these being natives of Hastings except eighteen." Professor Macoun adds:—"I could see nothing in the flora to lead me to doubt the feasibility of raising all the cereals in the valley of the Kaministiquia, a valley said by Professor Hind to contain an area of more than 20,000 acres exclusive of the Indian reservations." Nor is Professor Macoun at all singular in his estimate of the attractions of the Kaministiquia valley.

The Rev. George (now Professor) Grant, in his popular work[*] says of the same district:—"The flora is much the same as in our eastern provinces; the soil light, with a surface covering of peaty or sandy loam, and a subsoil of clay, fairly fertile and capable of being easily cleared. The vegetation is varied, wild fruits being especially abundant, raspberries, currants, gooseberries and tomatoes; flowers like the convolvulus, roses, a great profusion of asters, wild kallas, water lilies on the ponds, wild chives on the rocks in the streams, and generally a rich vegetation. It is a good country for emigrants of the farmer class. The road, too, is first-rate and the market is near. "The Valley of the Kaministiquia," he goes on to say, "is acknowledged to be a splendid farming country. Timothy grass was growing to the height of four feet on every vacant spot from chance seeds. A bushel and a half of barley, which was all a squatter had sown, was looking as if it could take the prize at an Ontario Exhibition." Thirty years before Professor Grant's visit, Sir George Simpson had been equally struck with the evidences of fertility of this region. He says:—[†]"The river (Kaministiquia) during the day's march passed through forests of elm, oak, pine, birch, &c., being studded with isles not less fertile and lovely than its banks; and many spots reminded us of the rich and quiet scenery of England. The paths of the portages were spangled with violets, roses, and many other wild flowers, while the currant, the gooseberry, raspberry, plum, cherry, and even the vine, were abundant. All this bounty of nature was, as it were, imbued with life by the cheerful notes of a variety of birds." Remembering that the country so enthusiastically described is contiguous to a mineral region of extraordinary richness, that the produce raised in the Valley of the Kaministiquia can be readily conveyed by water to the whole of the north or west shores of Lake Superior, and that the terminus of a transcontinental railway is close at hand with all the local demand that implies, little more need be said as to its attractiveness to the agricultural settler.

VALLEY OF THE MATAWIN.

Proceeding westward with Professor Macoun, we find him referring in the following terms to the Valley of the Matawin, a confluent of the Kaministiquia.

---

[*] Ocean to Ocean, p. 28.
[†] Overland Journey Round the World, 1841-2, Vol. 1, p. 36.

*" At the Matawin, vegetables of every description were growing luxuriantly, but more especially Timothy hay which seems to be peculiarly suited to the region round Thunder Bay. Many of the stalks were four feet in length with heads fully eight inches long. After passing the Matawin the soil changes to a reddish clay, but there is no change in the vegetation. The flora of the region indicates a moist climate, with a sufficiency of warmth to bring seeds in all cases to perfection. When the country becomes cleared up—which will be in a few years—either by accidental fires or by those of the settler, a marked change will take place in the climate. It will become drier and all kinds of grain will ripen much earlier. Coniferous trees, with a thick coating of moss, cover the greater part of the country; when these are gone a new crop of trees will spring up, but they will be deciduous ones, and the country will probably be less moist and warmer."

The Height of Land.

In the immediate vicinity of Lake Shebandowan there is little land fit for cultivation, but there is some fine land in the valleys and on the slopes in many places at no great distance, especially west of the Kashabowie Portage. There are scattered groups of red and white pine, but the principal forest growth is birch, oak, aspen, and scrub pine. The height of land is passed, and Lac des Mille Lacs is reached, surrounded with a continuous forest of spruce, balsam, aspen, and birch, with a sprinkling of red and white pine, and occasionally groups of Banksian pine. Baril Lake presents, according to Mr. Macoun, much the same characteristics as Lac de Mille Lacs.

A Pine Region.

But now the aspect of the country changes. On the shores of Lake Windegoostegon are large groves of red, white, and Banksian pine, the forest " taking the appearance of the pine lands of Ontario."† This continues till Pine Portage is reached, where "red and white pine attain to a great size, many of them being over three feet in diameter." As there are considerable areas of good land in the neighbourhood of Pine Portage, it may yet be the scene of a profitable conjunction of the lumbering and agricultural industries. From Pine Portage to Rainy Lake, and until the western end of the lake is reached, the country wears a cheerless aspect. Pine of good quality nearly disappears, but although little of it is fit for the saw-mill, vast quantities of railway ties might be produced, and easily shipped to Rat Portage. It will be borne in mind, however, that the foregoing applies only to one strip in a vast area of country, and that on the banks of the Seine and other rivers flowing into Rainy Lake, there is a very large growth of both red and white pine. The whole region, in fact, bounded by Lac Seul and English River on the north, and Lake of the Woods on the west, may be said to be a pine-growing territory.

---

* Report Canadian Pacific Railway, Appendix C, 1874.
† Professor Macoun's Report.

*RAINY RIVER.

We have now reached what, in an economical sense, is the most profitable and important section of the whole region lying between the height of land west of Lake Superior and the Lake of the Woods. Professor Macoun, speaking of his visit to the district, says :†—" The approach to Fort Frances is very beautiful. As we approach the outlet to the lake and enter Rainy River, the right bank appears very much like a gentleman's park, the trees standing far apart and having the rounded tops of those seen in open grounds. Blue oak (*Quercus Prinos var. discolor*), and Balsam Poplar (*Populus balsamifera*), with a few aspen, are the principal forest trees. These line the bank, and, for two miles after leaving the lake, we glide down between walls of living green, until we reach the Fort, which is beautifully situated on the right bank of Rainy River, immediately below the falls. All sorts of grain can be raised here, as well as all kinds of garden vegetables; little attention is given to agriculture, but enough was seen to show that nature would do her part if properly assisted. Barley, three feet high, and oats over that, showed there was nothing in the climate or soil to prevent a luxuriant growth. * * * The length of the river is about eighty miles. The right, or Canadian, bank, for the whole distance, is covered with a heavy growth of forest trees, shrubs, climbing vines, and beautiful flowers. The Indians say the timber gets larger as you proceed inland. The forest trees consist of oak, elm, ash, birch, basswood, balsam, spruce, aspen, balsam poplar, and white and red pine near the Lake of the Woods. The whole flora of this region indicates a climate very like that of central Canada, and the luxuriance of the vegetation shows that the soil is of the very best quality. Wild peas and vetches were in the greatest profusion; the average height was about six feet, but many specimens were obtained of eight feet and upwards. While the boat was wooding, I took a stroll inland, and found progress almost impossible, owing to the astonishing growth of herbaceous plants. The following plants were observed on Rainy River, and are only an index to the vast profusion of nature's bounties in that region :—Lilium Canadense, Lilium Philadelphicum, Vicia Americana, Calystegia spithamea, Calystegia sepium, Aralia hispida, Lobelia Kalmii, Smilacina stellata, Lathyrus venosus, Lathyrus ochrolencus, Monarda fistulosa, Viburnum pubescens, Astragalus Canadensis, Erysimum chieranthoides, Asarum Canadensis, and Lopaulthus anistatus." Writing of the Rainy Lake region, Sir George Simpson was fully as eulogistic of its merits and beauties as he had been of those of the Kaminiɡistiquia valley. His description agrees remarkably with that of Mr. Macoun just quoted : Sir George Simpson says :‡ " From Fort Francis downwards, a

---

* More properly René River its original name.
† Report, 1874.
‡ Overland Journey Round the World. 1841–2, p. 45.

stretch of nearly 100 miles, the river is not interrupted by a single impediment, while yet the current is not strong enough to retard an ascending traveller. Nor are the banks less favourable to agriculture than the waters themselves to navigation, resembling in some measure those of the Thames, near Richmond. From the very brink of the river there rises a gentle slope of green sward, crowned in many places with a plentiful growth of birch, poplar, beech, elm and oak. Is it too much for the eye of philanthropy to discern through the vista of futurity this noble stream, connecting as it does, the fertile shores of two spacious lakes, with crowded steamboats on its bosom and populous towns on its borders?" A few years later, before a Select Committee of the House of Commons in London, Sir George endeavoured to qualify to some extent, his former glowing panegyric. But he was at that time looking on this and some other matters in question, not with " the eye of philanthropy," but through a pair of Hudson's Bay monopoly spectacles, and, under a vigorous cross-examination by Mr. Roebuck, had virtually to admit the correctness of his first description, founded as it was on an experience of twenty-seven years.* The report of Mr. S. J. Dawson—now M. P. for Algoma—in 1874, and then engineer in charge of the district, fully corroborates the views of the two eminent authorities already quoted. He says:—" †Alluvial land of the best description extends along the banks of Rainy River, in an unbroken stretch of seventy-five or eighty miles from Rainy Lake to the Lake of the Woods. In this tract, where it borders on the river, there is not an acre unsusceptible to cultivation. At intervals there are old park-like, Indian clearings, partly overspread with oak and elm, which, although they have naturally sprung up, have the appearance of ornamental plantations. * * * The whole district is covered with forests, and Canadian settlers would find themselves in a country similar in many respects to the land of their nativity; nor does the climate differ essentially from that of the most favoured parts of Ontario or Quebec. Wheat was successfully grown for many years at Fort Frances, both by the old North-West Company and their successors, the Hudson's Bay Company. The Indians still cultivate maize on little farms on Rainy River and Lake of the Woods. In many places the wild grape grows in extraordinary profusion, yielding fruit which comes to perfection in the fall. Wild rice, which requires a high summer temperature, is abundant, and, indeed the flora, taken generally, indicates a climate in every way well adapted to the growth of cereals."

Supply of Pine Timber.

As regards the pine-growing capacities of this region, Mr. Dawson says‡:— " The Lake of the Woods receives the drainage of an area which may be approximately estimated at thirty-three thousand six hundred square miles, or 21,504,-

---

* Committee, House of Commons (G. B.) 1857, on Hudson's Bay Company.
† Public Works Report, 1874. Sessional papers (Canada), appendix 23.
‡ Public Works (Canada) Report. Appendix 23. Sessional Papers, 1875.

000 acres. In this vast district there are, of course, considerable varieties of climate, soil, and natural productions, but I desire expressly to draw attention to the fact, that it reaches nearly to the northern and north-western limits of the growth of pine wood of the class known, in Ontario and Quebec, as red and white pine ; that is, in the region eastward of the great prairies. Within this district, on the streams tributary to Rainy Lake, there are, in many places, extensive groves both of red and white pine, of a size and quality well adapted to all the purposes for which such timber is usually applied. On the alluvial belt of Rainy River white pine of a large size is to be seen interspersed with other descriptions of forest trees, and, on the Islands of the Lake of the Woods and main land to the north and east, there are occasionally pine groves of moderate extent; but, on proceeding to the north, by way of the Winnipeg, it gradually becomes more rare, until, on reaching Lake Winnipeg it finally disappears." In the region west of the Lake of the Woods, and thence to the Rocky Mountains, except at one or two isolated spots near the Lake, pine, properly so called, is unknown, and has to be imported by the ever-increasing population of Manitoba and the North-West. Lt.-Col. Dennis, lately Surveyor-General of the Dominion, and now Deputy Minister of the Interior, estimates the quantity of pine to be found between Lake Superior and the Lake of the Woods,—including that on the Islands in the Lake and within the region which may be supposed to be embraced between the International Boundary and the new boundary awarded to Ontario on the north—at twenty-six thousand millions of feet, board measure. All this is destined to be consumed in the Province of Manitoba and the North-West Territories. That it will form no unprofitable trade to the capitalist who embarks in it, may be judged from the fact that timber sells at the present time for from 25 to 45 dollars per thousand at Winnipeg. A cargo lately shipped from Collingwood, where it cost 10 dollars per thousand, was sold for 30 dollars in the Capital of Manitoba, and realized a good profit after paying all the charges for freight *via* Duluth and the Red River. From Fort Frances the cost of shipment to Winnipeg would be trifling, and, as the Lake of the Woods is too stormy for the transit of logs, the lumber must be manufactured in the district where it is found, thus giving a grand impetus to local industry and lake transportation. The foundations of such a trade have been already laid by the allotment, under Dominion authority, of extensive timber limits, and the establishment of a saw mill on a large scale at Fort Frances. A population of some 400 souls has been already attracted to the spot, and it is stated that some persons who had passed *via* Rainy River to Manitoba had returned and taken up land on Rainy River, owing to a preference for a well timbered country over one in which timber was scarce and dear.

ALBERTON.

The name of "Alberton" has been given to the settlement, which also rejoices in the possession of a local newspaper, the Alberton *Star*, in which appeared, during the present year, the following:—" The lots immediately fronting on the river are ten chains in width and have a depth of two miles; each settler is allowed to homestead one of these lots, and pre-empt the adjoining one, if vacant, also. About fifty entries have been taken here during the past summer, and considerable improvements have and are now being made on these lots. Some very fine crops were harvested by those who took the trouble to sow and plant in this section last season, samples of which may be seen at the land office here. To the industrious man, be he farmer, mechanic, or labourer, with a small capital, Rainy River presents an opening second to no other district in the Dominion of Canada—and where in a few years any such man may become independent. * * * * From Fort Frances to Rat Portage (about 120 miles) we have an excellent water route *via* Rainy River and the Lake of the Woods. There are upon these waters now one large side-wheel steamer, 'Lady of the Lakes,' and two tugs, with an addition probably of another large tug next season. Those vessels will pass down the whole length of Rainy River on their way out, and must consequently touch upon every man's homestead on the river, thus enabling him to take his produce to any market he pleases. In the meantime he may obtain a good price for anything he wishes to dispose of at Fort Frances or Rat Portage. At the former place there are now about sixty houses and 400 inhabitants—all necessary conveniences, four stores, post-office, school, blacksmith shop and church—and these have all arisen within three years. We have also Mr. Fowler's large saw mill, where you may get your lumber plain or dressed, doors, sashes, laths, shingles, etc. Mr. Fowler is further making arrangements for the importation of a grist mill, to run in connection with his saw mill, on the opening of navigation. * * * * We may also take into consideration the fact that the land on the opposite side of the river is quite as good as our own, and that the American Government will doubtless soon place it in the market. Our canal will shortly be completed, and through its gates the large lumbering trade (soon to be created) in the neighbouring State, Minnesota, must pass. This will add much to the trade and commerce of Rainy River." A later issue of the same paper speaks of the favourable crops of the present year, the busy demand upon the new grist mill, the establishment of a Hudson's Bay Company's post at Sturgeon Falls, the summer-like weather prevailing in the fall, the construction of another steamer for the Rainy River and Lake of the Woods navigation, the arrivals of several new settlers, and other signs of a healthy, growing, and prosperous community.

ADJACENT TERRITORY IN MINNESOTA.

As well remarked in the newspaper we have already quoted, it is not from the territory within Canadian jurisdiction alone that the Rainy River settlements are likely to derive advantage. While, from a distance of fully one hundred miles to the northward, the streams flow into Rainy Lake or River, and are thus made tributary to the trade and commerce of the settler in that district, the large area lying between the height of land in Minnesota to the southward, and Rainy River, is also capable of being rendered a prolific source of wealth. The height of land which divides the source of the Mississippi from the waters that ultimately find their course to Hudson's Bay lies nearly parallel to and some 60 to 70 miles south of Rainy River, about midway between that river and the Northern Pacific Railway from Duluth to the west. The country is said to be well timbered, to yield large quantities of pine, and to contain, in the neighbourhood of Lake Vermillion, rich mineral deposits. The Big Fork and Little Fork Rivers, emptying themselves into Rainy River, and the Vermillion River, falling into Nameukan Lake may all be utilized for conveying the timber and other products of Minnesota to a common focus at Fort Frances. That the settlers on the American side are alive to the advantages of traffic with Canada is shown by the following, clipped from the *Star* of October 29th:—" One of the settlers from the Minnesota side of Rainy River shipped a cargo of 300 bushels of potatoes to Rat Portage a short time ago, which he got sale for, as soon as landed, at prices ranging from seventy-five cents to one dollar per bushel. The same party has started with the second lot, which he has already disposed of, on his arrival at the Portage, to the railroad people."

Fort Frances Lock.

The works at Fort Frances consist of a canal 800 feet in length, cut through the solid rock, about forty feet wide, with one lift of 24 feet 8 inches. The chamber of the lock is 200 feet long and 38 feet wide in the clear. The lowest depth of water on the sills will be 5 feet 6 inches, but it is rarely if ever known to be so low as that, and is ordinarily from 8 to 10 feet. The cost of the works to the Dominion Government has been $250,000.

The Indians.

The relations of the Government and white population of the territory to the Indian tribes must, necessarily, be an object of considerable interest and importance. The Indians of the country lying between Lake Superior and the Lake of the Woods are Saulteux of the Ojibway nation. They derive their name from Sault Ste. Marie, from the neighbourhood of which they originally immigrated. In the southern division of the new territory they probably do not number over from 3,500 to 4,000 souls, nearly one-half of whom are settled in the vicinity of the Lake of the Woods and Rainy River.

Number Three Treaty.

These Indians, as well as some of the same tribe, settled on Lac Seul, are those embraced in what is known as Treaty Number 3, negotiated at the North-West Angle of the Lake of the Woods, in 1873, by Lieut.-Governor Morris, with

Messrs. S. J. Dawson and J. A. N. Provencher as joint Commissioners. This treaty settled any troubles or difficulties that had arisen out of the encroachments of Canadian settlers or surveyors on what the Saulteux had regarded as their lands. The negotiations afforded, too, a very excellent opportunity for testing the intelligence and general character of the tribe as there represented. Archbishop Taché, in his work,* deplores the persistency with which the Saulteux cling to their pagan faith, and the habits and customs incidental to their unconverted condition. But although so hostile to christianizing influences, the Saulteux of this region are not deficient in many of the qualities that command respect. They are brave, high-spirited, and among themselves, very capable of self-government. The bands at Rainy River and Lake of the Woods meet frequently in Council, discuss their affairs very intelligently, and enforce sternly the rules and regulations considered necessary for the common welfare. While mostly retaining the primitive wigwam, and practising pagan rites, they are far more thrifty, prudent, and industrious, than many of their race. In addition to the products of the shore, the lakes yield them an unlimited supply of fish, principally white fish and sturgeon—the extensive marshes produce immense quantities of wild rice, which the Indians collect on a systematic plan enjoined by their self-imposed laws, and the same plant attracts vast numbers of wild ducks of every description which divide with the Indians the collection and consumption of the rice, with, however, this advantage on the side of the Indian, that, while the ducks can only eat the rice, the Indian, in addition to the rice, can also eat the ducks. When first visited by missionaries, these Indians were already cultivating maize, which they still raise on their clearings, a proof, at once, of their partial civilization, and the favourable nature of the soil and climate of the district. The main body of the Saulteux refuse to hold communication with the small band at Pigeon River, whom they regard as an inferior class, and look with supreme contempt on the little settlement at Islington, where, under missionary guidance, a christianized population, fifty or more in number, have made good progress in the arts of civilized life, especially agriculture. The Saulteux are keen at bargains, and managed to make a very good one under the Treaty of 1873. Lieut.-Governor Morris gives an amusing account of the negotiations.† For four days they held aloof from meeting the commissioners altogether. On the fifth, they attended in response to a peremptory summons. It then appeared that jealousies among themselves were the chief cause of delay, and that, so fearful were they lest one chief or band should obtain an undue advantage over others by privately communicating with the Commissioners, that they had set a guard over the Lieut.-Governor's house and Mr. Dawson's tent. Several days were consumed in listening to and refusing exorbitant demands, until mat-

---

* Sketch of the North-West of America, p. 120.
† Sessional Papers (Canada) 1875. No. 8, p. 15.

ters at last came to a dead lock, and the Commissioners declared they would leave unless the Indians came to terms. "This," says the narrator, "brought matters to a crisis. The chief of the Lac Seul band came forward to speak. The others tried to prevent him, but he was secured a hearing. He stated that he represented four hundred people in the north; that they wished a treaty; that they wanted a schoolmaster to be sent them to teach their children the knowledge of the white man; that they had begun to cultivate the soil, and were growing potatoes and Indian corn, but wished other grains for seed and some agricultural implements and cattle." "This chief," says Mr. Morris, "spoke under evident apprehension as to the course he was taking in resisting the other Indians, and displayed much good sense and moral courage." He was supported, however, by Chief Blackstone, whose residence is at Pine Portage, and, the ice once broken, the business of the meeting went forward. But after some progress had been made, the spokesman of the Indians presented, with new demands, a request that fifty dollars annually should be paid to each chief, and a new suit of clothing for every member of the band was capped by the still cooler proposal that they should all have *free passes for ever over the Canadian Pacific Railway.* It will hardly be alleged, after this, that the Saulteux of North-western Ontario have not made exceedingly good progress in the manners and customs of their white exemplars.

Terms of the Treaty.

The Treaty provides for the cession of all the lands within the following boundaries:*—" Commencing at a point on the Pigeon River route where the International Boundary Line between the territories of Great Britain and the United States intersects the height of land separating the waters running to Lake Superior from those flowing to Lake Winnipeg; thence northerly, westerly, and easterly, along the height of land aforesaid, following its sinuosities whatever their course may be, to the point at which the said height of land meets the summit of the watershed from whence the streams flow to Lake Nepigon; thence northerly and westerly, or whatever may be its course, along the ridge separating the waters of the Nepigon and the Winnipeg to the height of land dividing the waters of the Albany and the Winnipeg; thence westerly and north-westerly, along the height of land dividing the waters flowing to Hudson's Bay by the Albany or other rivers, from those running to English River and the Winnipeg, to a point on the said height of land bearing north forty-five degrees east from Fort Alexander at the mouth of the Winnipeg; thence south forty-five degrees west to Fort Alexander at the mouth of the Winnipeg; thence southerly along the eastern bank of the Winnipeg to the mouth of the White Mouth River; thence southerly by the line described as in that part forming the eastern boundary of

---

* Sessional Papers (Canada), 1875, No. 8, p. 19.

the tract surrendered by the Chippawa and Swampy Cree Tribes of Indians, to Her Majesty, on the 3rd of August, 1871, namely, by White Mouth River to White Mouth Lake, and thence, in a line having the general bearing of White Mouth River to the forty-ninth parallel of North Latitude, to the Lake of the Woods, and from thence by the International Boundary line to the place of beginning."

A reference to the map* will show that this Treaty, consequently, covers three fourths of that portion of Ontario we have been describing as the western division of the territory embraced by the late arbitration. It extends, however, considerably beyond the boundaries of Ontario as assigned by the award, probably a little over one-third of the whole being north of the waters of Lac Seul and English River or west of the Lake of the Woods. The area, by the cession of which Ontario is directly benefited, is bounded by Lac Seul and English River on the north; by the Winnipeg River, Lake of the Woods, and International Boundary Line on the west; by the International Boundary Line on the south; and by the height of land which first separates the waters of Lac Seul from those of Lake St. Joseph (the head of the Albany River), and then those flowing eastward into Lake Superior, from those flowing to Lake of the Woods and forming the Dawson Route. The whole area ceded is stated to be 55,000 square miles,† and of this we may rightly estimate 35,000 as coming within Ontario jurisdiction. From this have to be taken the Indian Reserves, the allotments of lands for that purpose not to exceed one square mile for each family of five persons. The right of hunting is to be continued to the Indians, subject to such regulations as may be prescribed by law, or to the limitations imposed by settlement.

Subsidies and Presents.

The payments, in money or kind, made by way of purchase or presents, once for all, in return for the cession, were as follows:—‡Twelve dollars per head for every man, woman, or child belonging to the lands there represented; for every band who were then cultivating, or should hereafter cultivate, the soil, two hoes for every family actually cultivating; also one spade per family as aforesaid; one plough for every family as aforesaid; one scythe for every family as aforesaid; and also one axe and one cross-cut saw, and handsaw, one pit saw, the necessary files, one grindstone, one augur for each band; and also for each chief, for the use of his band, one chest of carpenters' tools; also for each band, enough of wheat, barley, potatoes, and oats, to plant the land actually broken up for cultivation by each band; also for each band, one yoke of oxen, one bull, and four cows. In addition to these gratuities, the sum of fifteen hundred dollars is to be spent annu-

---

* Map of North-west Territory, &c., exhibiting tracts ceded by Indian Treaties, accompanying Report of Minister of Interior, 1876.

† Lieutenant-Governor Morris's Report, Sessional Papers (Canada), 1875, No. 8, p. 18.

‡ Sess. Papers (Canada), 1875, No. 8, p. 20-21.

ally in the purchase of ammunition and nets for the Indians; a sum of five dollars per head is to be paid to each Indian also annually; each duly recognized chief is to receive a salary of twenty-five dollars per annum, and each subordinate officer —not exceeding three for each band—fifteen dollars per annum. Each chief and subordinate officer is also to be provided with a suit of clothing once in every three years. Finally, in recognition of the closing of the treaty, each chief received a flag and medal. Schools for instruction were also to be established wherever the Indians desired it, and all intoxicating liquors were to be excluded from the reserves.* In connection with the granting of the medals, an incident occurred during the conference, certainly creditable to the astuteness of the Saulteux, if not to their knowledge of the precious metals. Mawedopinias, the chief who acted as principal spokesman, who had obtained a medal given to one of the Red River chiefs, declared it was not silver, as it turned black, and, contemptuously striking it with his knife, protested he and his friends would he ashamed to wear it.

Progress in Civilization.

In the report of the Minister of the Interior for 1877 the following passage occurs: †—" The Indians who reside about eighty miles west of Rat Portage, within the limits of Treaty No. 3, are represented to be making satisfactory advancement in the arts of civilization, and stock-raising to some extent is ventured on; and altogether a commendable spirit of enterprise has developed itself among them. At Lac Seul, also, the progress of the Indians is said to be quite marked." The Indians west of Rat Portage are, of course, beyond the Ontario western boundary.

Numbers Included in Treaty No. 3.

The accounts of the Indian Department for 1877 show that the Indians receiving annuities under Treaty No. 3 numbered 2,890, classified as follows:— 9 Chiefs, 26 Headmen, 2,855 Indians. The annuities paid in 1877 amounted to $14,890; the total sum placed to the credit of the bands being $17,440. The tribe in this region counted not many years since 20,000 souls. Small-pox has reduced them to their present numbers.

Geological Features.

The reports of the Crown Lands Department of Ontario refer to the numerous mining locations granted within the area bounded on the west and north of Lake Superior by the height of land, and the whole of the interior region west of Lake Superior has been the subject of geological surveys, very full accounts of which have appeared in the reports of the Geological Branch of the Depart-

---

*ov. Morris' report, Sess. Papers (Canada), 1875, No. 8, p. 17.
†l Papers (Canada) 1875. No. 10. Report Deputy-Superintendent General, p. 15.

ment of the Interior.* That the geological conditions are indicative of valuable mineral deposits, there can be no doubt. A band of rocks running south-west from Lake Shebandowan—in the neighbourhood of which gold has been found in considerable quantities—to the Internaional Boundary, and thence to Lake Vermillion in Minnesota, is rich in auriferous deposits. Around Jackfish Lake they are probably most marked, but specimens of gold and gold ore are found along the whole line of country above indicated. The entire region, also, of the Rainy River invites further explorations. Mr. Dawson in his report (1874)† says:—"The Indians, both of Rainy Lake and Lake of the Woods have among them specimens of native gold and silver ore, which they affirm is to be found in places known to them in abundance, and the rock formation is such as to corroborate their statement. Iron ore is plentiful in many sections, and charcoal for smelting easily obtainable. Granite, which report says is equal in texture and fitness to the best imported specimens, is to be found at the Lake of the Woods, and the steatite, of which the Indians make pipes, a very valuable article for the construction of furnaces, is quite abundant at Rainy Lake and Sabaskin." It was stated in evidence before the Committee on Immigration and Colonization, at Ottawa, last year,‡ that coal had been discovered in the vicinity of Rainy River. There does not appear to be any reason, on scientific grounds, for doubting the existence of coal in that region, but its quality or the extent of the deposits, if they exist, are subjects for further inquiry before much reliance can be placed on the value of the alleged discovery.

The mineral resources of the district intervening between the height of land and Lake of the Woods must be mainly predicated upon the investigations of the geologist, and the information he supplies. Professor Robert Bell in a series of notes on the geological formation of the country on the line of the Dawson route, writes as follows:§—"Laurentian gneiss, running in a west south-westerly direction, extends from a point on the south shore of Lac des Mille Lacs, about four miles east of Baril Portage, all along the chain of lakes which this route follows as far as Sturgeon Lake. Mica Schist begins near the inlet of Sturgeon Lake, and continues along the route as far as Cross Lake. The Maligne and Island Portages occur in this interval. The Mica Schist appears to be all of the same character. It is moderately coarse-grained, and has a white shining appearance with black specks on fresh fracture, and often holds small hard patches of pebbles of a granular quartzose character like sandstone. At Cross Lake the Mica Schist becomes much mixed with reddish granite in the form of veins and intruded masses, the proportion of granite increasing in approaching Nequaquon Portage, at the western extremity of the Lake. In the western part of Cross Lake nearly all the points and islands are formed of

---

* Reports Geological Surveys (Canada), 1872-3, 1873-4, by Professor Bell.
† Public Works Report, 1875, Appendix 23.
‡ Report of Committee, page 139.
§ Geological Survey, 1873-4. p. 87.

granite. At Nequaquon Portage the rock consists of a dark grey mica schist, interstratified with gneiss, the latter prevailing towards the west end of the Portage where it has entirely replaced the former. * * * The rocks along the route from Nequaquon Portage towards Kettle Falls consist partly of gneiss and partly of a dark coarse splintery shining mica schist, to a point on Nemakon Lake, about six miles west of the narrows by which we entered it. Along the east side of Nequaquon Lake, and approaching the main body of gneiss in the western part of Nemakon Lake, the gneiss and mica schist are interstratified with each other, while between the two latter the rock consists of mica schist alone, with some veins and masses of granite. Proceeding westward from Kettle Falls through Rainy Lake, gneiss continues to prevail for about twenty miles. The gneiss at that locality holds micaceous bands and intruded waves of coarse reddish grey granite. . . . A broad band of schist covers the central part of Rainy Lake. This appears to be the same band which follows the Seine River, and is probably identical with the one which covers Bush Creek. The Indians at Fort Frances manufacture pipes from a grey slate, which occurs on the long point between the mouths of the Manitou and Seine Rivers. Mr. Robert Pither, the Indian Agent at Fort Frances, showed me specimens of light coloured granular iron pyrites, which, he informed me, were taken from a thick band in the same locality as the pipe-stone. I was shown a specimen of coarse silvery quartzose mica schist, which is said to occur, *in situ*, in the above neighbourhood. Mr. Pither likewise exhibited me a sample of copper pyrites in quartz from a vein on Rainy Lake, but he was not certain of the exact locality at which it occurs. He confirms the accounts of Mr. Dawson and others as to the occurrence of Huronian schists along the Seine River. The rock at the Falls of the Rainy River is a massive grey granitoid gneiss. Gneiss is also seen on the river about a mile below Fort Frances, and again at about ten miles. An expanse of massive-looking rocks, apparently Huronian schists, occurs at the mouth of Rapid River, which joins Rainy River from the southward, about fifteen miles from the Lake of the Woods. The banks of Rainy River, except on approaching the Lake of the Woods, are generally from fifteen to twenty feet high, and are composed of clay and drift materials, in which pebbles and boulders of a yellowish-grey limestone are plentiful. There is reason to believe, however, that, under these superficial deposits, a broad band of Huronian rocks covers the lower section of the river." The information thus afforded, while not absolutely conclusive, is so far indicative of mineral deposits of greater or less richness in the region we have been describing, as to suggest the propriety of a careful exploration, with the special object of ascertaining more thoroughly the value of the district for mining purposes. If to an abundance of splendid farming land, extensive pine forests, and a water way open to a market of which the demand will be unlimited, the country traversed by the Dawson route should develop the mineral resources indicated by its geolo-

Lac des Mille Lacs (via Lac Seul) to Winnipeg River.

gical formation, it will prove a rich acquisition both to the commerce of Ontario and the revenue of the Government.

While the exigencies of travel, and the need felt for a highway through Canadian territory to the North-West, have done much to further a knowledge of the features of the southern portion of the country we are describing, scientific explorations have been made along its northern limits by the officers of the Geological Survey. Starting from Lac des Mille Lacs, Messrs. Selwyn and Bell, in 1872, travelled by canoe the whole distance of 461 miles, to the Winnipeg River, encountering no more serious obstacles than portages, which were easily crossed, or the danger of being lost in the labyrinthine system of lakes, streams, and rivers, with which the whole route is more or less intersected.* A very brief sketch of the journey condensed from the published reports, will give a fair idea of the nature of the country visited. Leaving Lac des Mille Lacs on the 29th of August, the party, on the 10th September, were camped on Sturgeon Lake, having passed over twenty-five portages, altogether 9,836 yards in length, in a distance of 100 miles. Being deserted by their Indians, the travellers fortunately recruited their force by the voluntary services of half a dozen Pacific Railway surveyors' men, who were met with on the way, and who desired to return to their homes on Red River. On the 16th of September the camp was on the line of the Railway Survey, from which point the Sturgeon Lake River was descended about ten miles, to the head of the second rapids in the portage, 210 yards in length. A journey of four miles further, brought them to the falls by which Sturgeon Lake River discharges into Lake Minnietaki, there being in that distance three portages, respectively 1,500, 250, and 1,280 yards in length. The water, however, was then at its lowest stage; when the river is full the rapids may be descended in a canoe. It is between Minnietaki Lake and Lac Seul that the route becomes most intricate, and, but for the fortunate appearance of a wandering Indian, who acted as pilot, the journey might have had a premature ending. One portage, 1,758 yards in length, being crossed, the canoes entered a small river flowing directly into Lac Seul, and on the 20th September, the Hudson's Bay Company's Post on that lake was reached, 81 miles from the camp on Sturgeon Lake, the trip in that distance involving portages, thirteen in number, and aggregating 7,848 yards in length. The Hudson's Bay Post, on Lac Seul, appears from the maps to be situated about midway between the eastern and western extremities of the lake. Some idea of the extent of this sheet of water may be formed from the fact that, from the post to the head of the English River, at the western end of the lake, the distance is 52 miles. The passage down the English River to its junction with the Winnipeg, was accom-

---

* Geological Survey, 1872-3, p. 87.

plished by the 2nd of October, the portages to be crossed being twelve in number, and measuring altogether 5,535 yards.

As to the general aspect of the country, Professor Selwyn, after urging the importance of a mineralogical survey of "the great parallel bands of schistose and slaty strata traversing this region," and pointing out that gold, copper, and iron, are associated with similar strata, says:—* " Except such as arises from causes connected with the presence of Huronian rocks, as above described, or with the occurrence of superficial deposits of sand clay, &c., but little variation is perceived in the general aspect of the country, on the route which we traversed, between Lac des Mille Lacs and Lake Winnipeg. On the mainland, and on the innumerable islands, the shores of the lakes and rivers, generally present bare rock surfaces. Bold cliffs and precipices are rare; the rocks either rise abruptly from the water for fifteen or twenty feet, or else slope gently upward, till, above the line of highest flood, they are concealed beneath a thin coating of moss-covered soil, supporting a thick undergrowth of brushwood, and a forest of poplar, aspen, birch, spruce, and small tamarack, with, occasionally, a few red pine trees, standing singly or in small clumps, and which, though considerably taller than the rest of the forest, and hence conspicuous at a distance, are rarely of large size. The generally small size of the timber, however, is evidently not altogether due to the effects of unfavourable soil and climate, but in a great measure to the fact that nearly all the older trees have been destroyed by the successive fires that at one time or other have devastaed every part of the country, and the effects of which are often conspicuously marked by the tall dead branches and charred trunks which still tower above the younger forest. There are no prominent hills or even ridges; the highest elevations do not probably exceed four or five hundred feet above the intervening waters, and I think it is no exaggeration to say that the latter occupy fully one half of the whole surface area of the region. The surface is generally undulating and broken, and often rocky, but occasionally both lakes and rivers are bordered either by extensive swampy flats, or by banks of stratified sand, silt, and clay, which ofter rise terrace-like at a short distance from the water's edge. The point on which the Hudson Bay Company's Post stands is formed of these deposits, and to the westward of the Post, along the north shore, they are exposed in cliff sections for several miles. At the junction of the Mattawa and English Rivers, where a small Indian village and trading post is situated, presided over by Chief Pierre, there are similar banks of sand and sandy clay resting on the ordinary grey Laurentian gneiss, which is exposed along the water's edge. The banks here rise steeply to about thirty feet above the water, and for some distance inland the country seems to be tolerably level, and the soil on this part of the river appears to be generally of fair quality. Small patches of it are cultivated by the Indians, who succeed in raising excellent

---

* Geological Survey, 1872-3, p. 16.

potatos, carrots, and onions, and there is no doubt that many crops would flourish equally well, and would be cultivated by them if they were supplied with seed. Throughout the region, especially from Sturgeon Lake westward to Lake Winnipeg, there are considerable areas of soil suitable for cultivation.

The Line of the Canadian Pacific Railway.

Following the course of the Canadian Pacific Railway, as located and partially constructed between Fort William and Rat Portage, on the Lake of the Woods, we gather a fair idea of the character of the country from the reports of the engineers.*

From Fort William to Lacs des Mille Lacs the route has already been described. From thence to the arm of English River, crossed by the railway 113 miles from Thunder Bay the ground is slightly undulating, and although there are several rock cuttings they are generally in short lengths. Still their frequent presence denotes a rugged and uninviting surface. From the 113th to the 160th mile, where Little Wabigoon River is reached, the country is rolling, containing numerous lakes and swamps with very irregular rocky ridges. From Little Wabigoon to Thunder Lake, the latter 206 miles west from Thunder Bay, the country is very slightly undulating, but where excavations occur they will be in rock. For the next 58 miles the line traverses a heavy rolling country with numerous lakes, swamps and rocky hills and some good land interspersed. Lastly, from the 264th mile to the 298th at Rat Portage, the section is over a very rough rocky country, indented with numerous lakes and hollows and containing very little soil. It is evident that the route for the railway has thus far been chosen with an eye mainly to engineering purposes and objects, and, probably, to secure as the primary desideratum the most direct line to the Red River, but uninviting as the section it covers may appear from these descriptions, it must not be forgotten that the very fact of a railway passing through it gives value to what would otherwise be a waste, and justifies an expenditure of labour and capital in places, that without it, would never entice either to attempt their reclamation. Should mineral wealth be developed on the line of the railway route, as there is good reason to anticipate, it will not be long before whatever portions of the country can be made cultivable will be discovered and appropriated.

The Climate.

The ability, not only to live, but to enjoy life, in an atmosphere that, to the inhabitants of warm or very temperate regions appears to be almost incredibly severe, is tested every day for several months in the year by the hardy population of Canada. A very low temperature has few terrors, and is often attended with less actual suffering, or inconvenience, than the raw, damp, chilliness of a

---

* Canadian Pacific Railway Report, 1877. Appendix Z, p. 357 *et seq.*

milder climate. By no one need the western portion of North-Western Ontario be really dreaded. Mr. Sandford Fleming, in his Report of Progress, laid before Parliament in 1874, referring to the climatic peculiarities of the regions traversed by the Canadian Pacific Railway, says :—*" Throughout the whole of the woodland region (Nipissing to Red River), the depth of snow is generally less on an average than it is at the City of Ottawa. Only in one locality on the routes favourable for the railway, between Manitoba and Lake Nipissing, is the snow found generally so deep as at this city (Ottawa). The locality referred to is in the immediate neighbourhood of Lake Superior, where the route approaches the coast; here the lake appears to have a local influence on the humidity of the atmosphere, and, in consequence, on the amount of snow-fall. * * * From Lake Nepigon to Manitoba the snow ranges from 70 to less than 50 per cent. of the depth at Ottawa." A witness examined by the Committee on Colonization and Immigration, at Ottawa, in reply to a question respecting the climate of the Rainy River region, replied that it was " similar to Manitoba."† This statement would probably apply to the larger portion of the country the character of which we are now considering. The intensity of cold will, of course, vary according to the elevation or sheltered position of different localities. The Hon. Senator Sutherland, of Manitoba, before the above-named committee, in 1876 said, with regard to the winters in that Province :—‡" The frost penetrates on exposed places to the depth of from three to four feet, that is where the land is not covered at all with snow. Where it is covered with snow it is seldom frozen deeper than eighteen inches. Vegetation begins and progresses before the frost is all out of the ground, and we generally begin sowing when it is thawed to the depth of six inches, at which time the surface is perfectly dry. We believe this frost helps the growth of crops, owing to the heat of the sun by day, causing a continual evaporation from the underlying strata of frost. * * * We have occasional (summer) frosts; generally one frost about the first of June, but seldom severe enough to do any material injury to the growing crops, and showers are frequent during spring and summer. The average depth of snow throughout Manitoba is about 20 inches, and is quite light and loose." That the winter does not, in the region between Lake Superior and Lake of the Woods, encroach to an inconvenient extent upon the open season, is incidentally shown by a circumstance alluded to by Mr. Dawson, in his report to the Government of the Dominion, in 1874.§ At the close of the season of 1873, orders were suddenly received to prepare for the transportation of a body of the Mounted Police over the Dawson route. By the time the force had reached the north-west angle, winter had set in with great severity, and the result was, that a large force of workmen, em-

---

* Report Canadian Pacific Railway, 1874, p. 34 *et seq.*
†₊Report, p. 169. Journals House of Commons (Canada), 1878.
‡ Report of Committee, p. 39, Journals House of Commons (Canada), 1876.
§ Public Works Report, 1874. Appendix 23. Sess. Papers (Canada), 1875.

ployed in the transportation service, were winter bound. It is in making this statement Mr. Dawson incidentally mentions that the smaller lakes near the height of land were frozen over on the night of the 28th October, and that, although every effort was made to keep the navigation open, the thermometer fell on the night of the 2nd November, to 6° (Fahrenheit), completely stopping the tugs "But," he adds, " winter had set in earlier than ever before known in the short experience of the white man, or even in the knowledge of the Indians." In the report of the same gentleman to the Legislative Assembly of Canada, in 1858, he says :* Blodget, in his isothermic chart, shewing the mean distribution of heat for the summer, places the line of 60° to the north of the Lake of the Woods, and that of 65° at Fort Garry. * * * That a great precipitation of rain takes place at and near the highlands which separate the waters flowing to Lake Winnipeg, from those that run towards Lake Superior, is evinced by the magnitude of the rivers, as compared with the area they drain. The climate, however, seems to be milder on the western slope of the highlands than on the eastern." The following record, by Sir John Richardson, of the progress of the seasons at Fort William, will give some idea of the climatic conditions on the more favourably situated western slope of the height of land above referred to :†—

Feb. 9.—Thermometer at noon, 39° F.
March 1.—Temperature, 61° in the middle of the day.
April 2.—The sap of the sugar maple began to run.
" 9.—First wild ducks seen.
" 10.—Butterflies, blueflies, and gulls noticed.
" 20.—General thaw commences. Ground frozen to a depth of 3 ft. 9 in.
" 30.—River Kaministiquia partially open.
May 2.—River free of ice.
" 10.—The birch tree and maple budding.
June 15.—Swallows building.
July 15.—Barley just coming into ear. Potatoes in flower.
" 31.—Raspberries ripening.
Aug. 8.—Red currants and blueberries perfectly ripe.
" 19.—Barley ripening.
" 29.—Peas quite ripe.
" 31.—Swallows have disappeared.
Septr. 7.—Leaves of birch and aspen change colour.
" 13.—Potatoes, cabbage, turnips and cauliflowers nipped by frost.
October 7.—Leaves of the birch and aspen falling.
Nov. 3.—Small lakes frozen over.

---

* Journals Leg. Assembly, Canada, 1858. Appendix 36.
† Arctic Exploring Expedition, Vol. II., p. 227-8.

Nov.   9.—River covered with a sheet of ice, which broke up again.
Dec'ber 1.—Ice driving about by wind.
"   17.—Thunder Bay frozen across to the Welcome Islands.*

Another authority states that the average period of the Kaministiquia freezing over is from the 3rd to the 15th of November, and that it becomes free from ice between the 20th and 23rd of April. Bearing in mind the tendency to an amelioration of the climate in pursuing a westerly course, and the comparison instituted between the Rainy River region and Manitoba, there certainly are no climatic difficulties in the way of the colonization of the country lying between Lake Superior and the Lake of the Woods.

EASTERN DIVISION.

LAKE SUPERIOR TO JAMES BAY.

The possession of the territory lying north of the height of land and extending to the shores of Hudson's Bay opens up an entirely new field to energy and enterprise. The southern shore of the Bay, which forms under the late award the northern limits of Ontario jurisdiction, is but little further from Toronto than the City of Quebec; a railway from the present termination of our northern lines to Moose Factory need be accounted a no more chimerical scheme than would the proposition have been considered to connect Toronto with the ancient capital of the Lower Province by a similar means fifty years ago; and the terrors of frost and snow that, somehow or other, are associated in men's minds with the Hudson's Bay region, are certainly not more appalling than were the stories of hardship and suffering supposed, as but yesterday, to attach to a settlement in what is now the populous and busy capital of Manitoba. The broad rivers that flow northward and eastward into James or Hudson's Bay, seem to invite the voyager by the facilities they offer for his journey to the great northern sea or inland lake whose coasts he may desire to explore, and the head waters of our St. Lawrence or lake navigation, approach near enough to make the journey one of comparative ease to men inured to the experiences of Canadian pioneer life. These rivers could all tell a tale of strange doings in past times to which their waters have been witness; when Hudson's Bay Company's retainers contended for the rights secured to them under their monopoly; when their traders were intercepted by rivals by whom, and towards whom, rough measures were by no means repudiated; when the "French from Canada," outbid the Company's factors for the Indians' hunting spoils, and bore them away hundreds of leagues overland instead of leaving them to find their way by the annual ship from York Factory to Europe. To-day, when all strifes and hostile competition are at an end, the In-

* Journals Leg. Assembly (Canada), 1858. Appendix 3.

dians and trappers still bear their skins by the York, the Albany, or the Moose, to the respective Forts, and it is but some thirty years since a force of British troops, with ordnance, and accompanied by women and children, made a safe passage, by the Hayes river, from York Factory to Norway House, and thence by Lake Winnipeg and the Red River to Fort Garry, reaching their destination in thirty days. The country constituting what we shall call the western half of North Western Ontario, will be bounded by an imaginary line drawn north-west from the point at which the height of land, north of Lake Nepigon dips to the southward, to the head of Lake St. Joseph, the source of the Albany river. Thence easterly along that river to its mouth, thence east along the south shore of James Bay, nearly to its south east angle, then south along the boundary line between Ontario and Quebec, and finally westward along the height of land on the north of Lake Superior and Lake Nepigon, until the starting point is reached. But in order to estimate properly the value of the possession of this region, it will be necessary to take into consideration the trade and resources of the country lying north of the Albany, its connections with the trade of the North-west and also the promise of advantages accruing from a traffic in the products of Hudson's Bay itself. We shall first notice, however, the means and routes by which the Bay is accessible from the settled portions of Ontario or other parts of the Dominion.

ROUTES TO HUDSON'S BAY.

Several large rivers flow into James Bay, which is simply a contraction of Hudson's Bay at its southern extremity. From the south come the South Branch of the Moose, or the Mattagami, as it is called in the country, the Missinibi or North Branch of the Moose,—both streams uniting before discharging themselves into the Bay,—the Abbitibbe River coming from the south-east, which also joins the Moose and seeks its outlet at the same point; the Albany from the south-west, which enters the Bay about one hundred miles west of the Moose; the Harricanaw, which crosses the provincial boundary line some distance south of the Bay from the east; the Notaway and Rupert's River which are wholly to the eastward of that boundary, and enter the Bay at points on its south-eastern shore corresponding very nearly to the position of the mouths of the Moose and Attinibee on its south-western coast; and, further north still, the East Main or Slude River entering the Bay at a point nearly opposite the mouth of the Albany. Following the western shore of Hudson's Bay to the northward we first come to the Severn River, and then still further north to the Nelson and its southern Branch the Hayes River, at the mouth of which York Factory is situated. The Nelson river forms the channel by which the drainage of the whole region of the Lake of the Woods, fed by innumerable rivers and streams, of Lake Winnipeg which receives the waters of the Lake of the Woods, of the

Winnipeg, Red, and Assiniboine rivers, and of the mighty Saskatchewan with its confluents, find their way to the ocean. North of the Nelson is the Churchill, a large river, and still further to the north the Seal River. It is in the rivers of the south and west we are primarily interested in connection with our present inquiries. Recent explorations made under the direction of the Dominion Government have afforded very ample information as to the routes to James Bay through what is now, under the award, Ontario territory, from the south and south-west. A brief description of each survey will present a tolerably clear view of the general character of the country and the routes traversed.

Lake Huron to Moose Factory.

Setting out from the north shore of Lake Huron by way of the White-fish River, the Wanapiti River and Lake, Professor Bell, in 1865,* passed, by way of the Sturgeon River—which flows into Lake Nipissing and must not be confounded with a river of the same name west of Lake Superior,—through a succession of lakes to the head of the east branch of the Montreal River, a tributary of the Ottawa; thence *via* Pigeon Lake to Grassy River, the waters of which flow northwards to Lake Shatagami. From this lake, by a six mile portage, Lake Mattagami was reached, and a passage down the Mattagami to the south Branch of the Moose or Mattagami River effected. The river was surveyed to its junction with the north branch of the Moose or Missinibi. The party then passed down the main stream to Moose Factory a short distance south of the mouth of the river and open bay. Mattagami Lake, which gives the river its name, and which, if not *the* source, may be regarded as one of its sources, is about 26 miles in length. For five or six miles the river, after leaving the lake, flows smoothly but then takes a plunge, first by a fall, and then a rapid, thus accomplishing a descent of forty-five feet. This impediment to navigation is overcome by a portage known as Fishing Portage, a mile in length, on the west side of the river. At a distance of a mile and a half from Fishing Portage the river enters Kenogamissee Lake, twenty-two miles in length. The united length of the two lakes and intervening river supplies a navigation of some fifty-four miles with one portage a mile long as the sole interruption. From the foot of Kenogamisse Lake to Moose Factory is a distance of 216½ miles, divided as follows:—

From Kenogamissee Lake to a (first) brook at a S. E. bend about N. E.	12 miles.
To second brook at a N. E. bend about N.	3 "
To a third brook to a S.W. bend about W.	5 "
To Muckwa Powitik (Bear Rapid), about N.	66 "

---

* Geological Survey, 1875-6, p. 294.

To foot of Long Portage to junction of Missinibi Branch,
about N. 42 deg. E.. 39½ miles.
From junction of Missinibi to Moose Factory, about N.
52 deg. E... 46 "

Total .... 216¼ miles.

Long Portage is the last of eighteen portages in the above distance. It is four miles in length, and avoids a descent of 190 feet, the three portages above it being represented by a fall in the river of 195 feet. Adding forty feet for the intervening space the total descent in 10 miles is 425 feet. On leaving Kenogamissee Lake the river falls some 117 feet in three-quarters of a mile, but the intervening portages are described as "short, with a comparatively slight fall in the river at each," so slight, in fact, that canoes can be frequently taken up and down with a half load. Numerous streams help to swell the Mattagami in its northward course the principal one, besides the Missinibi, already mentioned, being the Abbitibbe which joins the Mattagami 17 miles south of Moose Factory. The most interesting fact, perhaps, in the foregoing brief sketch of the Mattagami's course is he existence of a stretch of ninety miles inland from James Bay, with no serious impediment to navigation whatever.

Moose Factory to Michipicoton.

Leaving the topographical and productive features of the country watered by the Mattagami, to be noticed subsequently, we will now turn southward and accompany Mr. Bell on his homeward trip, his objective point being the River Michipicoton on Lake Superior, probably the nearest point on the navigable waters of the St. Lawrence chain to James's Bay, and which, owing to the wide reach of country, extending from Lake Huron northwards, before the height of land is crossed, and the sources of the Moose are reached, must, in the absence of roads or railroads be one of the more natural and accessible routes to Hudson's Bay.* We have already traced the Mattagami or South Branch of the Moose to its union with the North Branch or Missinibi and thence to James Bay at Moose Factory. The return trip will therefore commence at the junction of the two streams. In a straight line the distance from Round Bay 4½ miles below Long Portage to the outlet of Missinibi Lake is 113 miles. Following the course of the river the distance is much greater. The portages, twenty in number, are as follows:—

1. Long portage... 1 mile.
2. Storehouse portage .... ½ "
3. Congening House portage....... .... 866 paces.

---

* Geological Survey, 1875-6, p. 327.

4. River side portage...................... 673 paces.
5. Kettle portage .... 100 yards.
6. Black feathers portage................ ¼ mile.
7. Rocky Island portage .... 160 paces.
8. Sandy Bay portage .... 85 "
9. Sharp rock portage .... 87 "
10. Beaver portage .... 455 "
11. Sugar loaf portage................... 77 "
12. Pond portage. Length not stated.
13. A portage sometimes navigable ...... 200 "
14. St. Paul's portage .... 178 "
15. St. Peter's portage .... 330 "
16. Okandago (or Greenhill) portage.....1634 "
17. Wavy portage........................ 110 "
18. Island portage .... 431 "
19. Foot-of-swampy-grounds portage ..... 353 "
20. Keg portage .... 360 "

In the interval between the outlet of Missinibi Lake and the mouth of the Michipicoton there are seven more portages. Following the general course of each of the stretches above-given, the total distance from Moose Factory to the mouth of the Michipicoton is 314 miles, or in a straight line 281¼ miles. In round figures it may therefore be said that, at this point, the waters of Lake Superior are separated from those of Hudson's Bay by a distance of a little over 300 miles. The number of portages varies considerably with the season and the state of the rivers and their feeders. In many cases, with a light load the rapids can be wholly overcome, and a recourse to portaging avoided.

Missinibi Lake is a fine sheet of water twenty-four miles in length and at about eighteen miles from the outlet a bay opens off the north-east side and runs back north-east parallel to the main body of the lake about nine miles. "On the south-east side of the lake fifteen miles from the outlet," says the report, "a river falls a considerable height over the rocks into the lake. It is called Wi-a-sitch-a-wan or "Water shining from Afar." The country traversed by the Missinibi must be of a generally level character, for, according to Mr. Bell, the first hills seen from the river after leaving Moose Factory were immediately north of Missinibi Lake. It is doubtful, however, whether either of the two routes above described is the true one, if the object be to secure the easiest means of access to the waters of Hudson's Bay from the great lakes. A more advantageous route will probably be one from the north shore of Lake Nepigon to the main stream of the Albany, or, still better, one from the mouth of Black River on Lake Superior by way of Long Lake, and a southern branch of the Albany, joining the main river at about 150 miles from its mouth.

BLACK RIVER (LAKE SUPERIOR) TO THE ALBANY.

This route appears from the information at command, to possess the greatest natural advantages. After curving round Lake Nepigon the height of land dips suddenly to the southward, forming a sharp bend—or rather loop, for it immediately recedes to the northward again—opposite to the mouth of the Black River. In this loop, or bend, lies Long Lake, a narrow sheet of water fifty miles in length, its southern end being one mile north of the height of land, and only twenty-two miles from Lake Superior. Between the height of land and Lake Superior water communication exists; the Black River being navigable by light canoes for its whole length. But, as portaging would be necessary at several places for heavy freights, and as there is an intervening space between the waters running north and south respectively, which must, in any case, be overcome, it is possible that, whenever a scheme is devised for utilizing the navigation of Long Lake as a route to Hudson's Bay, the first effort will be to secure an easy method of land conveyance from Lake Superior to the nearest long stretch of navigable water. Although the country on the north coast of Lake Superior is generally rugged and rocky, the Canadian Pacific engineers who have surveyed a line of railway from Lake Nipissing to Nepigon River, which passes between the height of land south of Long Lake and Lake Superior, do not represent this section as being at all particularly formidable from their point of view, although they would traverse it longitudinally, while a road, tramway, or railroad, from Lake Superior to Long Lake, would cut it laterally. The elevation of Summit Portage is given by Mr. Bell as 489 feet above the Lake Superior level, while Long Lake is 466 feet above Lake Superior. From Long Lake with its fine stretch of fifty miles of clear navigation, flows the Kenogami River, marked as English River on some of the maps, but that name is appropriated by so many other streams, that it will be more convenient to use the Indian designation.

As considerable interest may attach to this route, it may be well to describe the Kenogami in Mr. Bell's own words. He says:—* "Leaving Long Lake the Kenogami River winds for two miles among open marshes, on which the Hudson Bay Company's men cut hay for the use of the cattle at Long Lake House; the general course of the river for the first nine miles is N. 10° E. In this section the first portage occurs at three, and the second at seven miles down, and between them on the west side, Kenogamishish, or little Long Lake River, enters at five, and Manitou-namaig, or Devil-Fish River, at six miles from Long Lake. From the outlet to the first of these tributaries, the river is only from a chain and a half to two chains wide; but below them it expands to four chains. Further down it continues to increase in width, till, at the end of nine miles (following the stream), from Long Lake, it averages ten or twelve chains. At the end of nine miles from

---

* Geological Survey, 1870-1; p. 338.

Long Lake, the river bends round, running N. 86° E. in a straight line for eight miles; then it enters the west side of Mani-gwa-ga-mi or Pine Lake at right angles about two miles from its southern extremity. Portages 3 to 7 occur in this stretch, and a river enters from the north. The main body of Pine Lake, which runs N. 12° E. is about seven and a half miles long, and one and a half wide. At a mile and a half from its northern extremity, a channel, ten chains wide, leads into the lower division of the lake. This runs N. 25° E., and is three and a quarter miles long and one mile wide. About one and a half miles from Pine Lake we reach the eighth portage, and immediately below it, Arm Lake, which is about three miles long and lies at right angles to the general course of the river. The ninth portage is passed at about two miles below Arm Lake; and half a mile further on, the river enters Ka-pees-a-watan Lake; two miles long in which there are several low islands. Mani-gwa-ga-mish or Little Pine River, flowing from a lake of the same name, enters the south side of this lake, and the Wa-big-a-no or Mouse River, comes in from the same side, about two miles in a straight line below the lake. A third stretch of the river which has a nearly east course below Pine Lake, terminates with a rapid a mile and a half long. This is avoided by a portage (the eleventh), the tenth one being a mile higher up. The fourth reach of the Kenogami river bears N. 45° E., and is thirteen and a half miles long in a direct line. It embraces portages twelve to seventeen, and terminates on the eighteenth, which is the last to the junction of the river with the Albany, on which canoe navigation is uninterrupted to the Bay. The Atick or Deer River enters from the north, between the sixteenth and seventeenth portages. The fifth reach bears N. 80° E., and was followed for twenty-one miles, when we reached Pembina Island, which although not large, is easily recognised by a conspicuous light-coloured bank about thirty-five feet high, running for about a mile along the north side of the river, immediately above it. Throughout this last stretch the river is shallow, swift, and sometimes rapid. In the last twelve miles explored, it spreads in several places among low islands, and flat lying limestone is exposed in the bed of the river. In the same interval it receives the Mun-did-i-no and Wa-tis-ti-gum Rivers from the north, and the Pe-wo-na or Flint River from the south. The following register is given of the portages on Kenogami River:—

	Chains.	Fall in River.		
1.	14	20	feet.	Trail level and dry. Carry canoes.
2.	5	7	"	Trail level and dry. Wade light canoes.
3.	12	22	"	Banks of gravelly earth. Carry canoes.
4.	9	25	"	Burnt land. Sandy trail. Wade light canoes.
5.	6	12	"	Run light canoes.
6.	3	4	"	Run light canoes.
7.	34	24	"	Steep bank at lower end. Carry canoes.
8.	4	3	"	Run light canoes.
9.	2	10	"	Over rocks. Carry canoes.

	Chains.	Fall in River.		
10.	6	12	"	Lower end steep and rocky. Carry canoes.
11.	120	75	"	Trail level but intersected with a few small ravines. Steep bank near lower end. Soil yellow clay, overlaid by gravelly loam. Carry canoes.
12.	1	7	"	Over rock. Carry canoes.
13.	5	10	"	Over rock. Carry canoes.
14.	12	15	"	Level trail. Run light canoes.
15.	5	6	"	Level trail. Carry canoes.
16.	25	20	"	Level trail. Wade, full canoes.
17.	4	6	"	Level trail. Wade, light canoes.
18.	1	4	"	Numerous small islands of gneiss in river. Run full canoes down. Wade up.

With the exception of a few rocky ridges and knolls in the upper part of the river, the country through which the Kenogami flows to join the Albany River, is uniformly level. Terraces or banks of brown loam and gravelly earth from ten to forty feet in height are to be seen all along the Kenogami and around Pine Lake, sometimes close to, and at others a short distance from the banks. The soil in the neighbourhood of the river is good. The timber is principally spruce, balsam-fir, white-cedar, tamarack, white-birch and aspen. Some of the larger spruces and tamaracks have been found to measure as much as from four to five feet in girth, at five feet from the ground, but the average diameter of the trees is about eighteen inches. As the last twenty or thirty miles is reached, the ground becomes swampy, the trees diminishing in size, and value in proportion. The distances from Lake Superior to James Bay by this route would be made up as follows:

Lake Superior to Long Lake	22	miles.
Long Lake free navigation, about	54½	"
Kenogami River and Lakes on its course	90¾	"
Pembina Island to junction of Kenogami with Albany	99	"
Albany to James Bay	150	"
	416¼	"

The route from Pembina Island to the junction with the Albany and thence to James' Bay, is without portages, and admits of canoe navigation. It would, however, be more correct to say that the Albany to the point of junction is fitted for navigation by larger craft, a fact that has been well-known ever since the earliest opening of the Hudson's Bay Company's trade. It was at this point that Henly House, or Fort, was erected, to protect the trade of the Company against the attempts of the French Canadians to intercept the Indians coming from the west to trade their furs and peltries at Albany, and not a few sharp encounters took place between the rivals, who in a limited scale, thus maintained a warfare, too often raging on a far more extensive one between the representatives of their respective nations nearer home. To the capabilities of the Albany for navigation as described by those who have tested them more recently, older authorities also bear testimony. Before a committee of the British House of Commons in 1749* one John Hayter, a servant of the Hudson's Bay Company, gave the following evidence: He said, "that he had been twelve days' journey up the Albany River to a Fort or Factory called Henly House, which is 150 or 200 miles up that River, that he saw large trees there but no corn." Being asked the occasion of building Henly House, he said "that the old leading Indian had been used ill by the Governor (at Albany) and brought four French Indians (Indians favourable to the French) from the Southerly to the Westerly River; upon which the Governor erected that Fort to prevent the French trade, who never traded there before that season." The Indians referred to had probably taken a route similar to the one we have just been discussing on the authority of Mr. Bell. The witness Hayter goes on to say: "that the climate is much warmer at Henly House than at Albany; but they broke no ground there and consequently he can give no account of the frost; that they carried up nothing but utensils and met with but few falls of waters (rapids) which they towed their boats up. That they were forced to row almost all day long, the stream being too rapid for boats to sail up even in a fresh gale; that it is impossible to tow the boats with horses on account of the badness of the ground, but one man tows a canoe of 24 or 25 feet long and 4 feet wide, which draws about eight inches of water and will carry a great weight; **** that the country about Henly House is very high but warmer than the coast; *** that he has seen large tracts of land that would, in his opinion, bear corn, (grain) if cultivated, the climate being much warmer within land." Long Lake being at a level of 466 feet above, and Pembina Island 120 feet below, the level of Lake Superior, a difference of only 586 feet in a distance of 140 miles, a road from the outlet of Long Lake to the point on the Kenogami which would be uninterrupted by portages would hardly be a work involving much labour or cost, if, indeed, it were not economical to construct it to the waters of the Albany itself.

LAKE NEPIGON TO ALBANY.

We have, however, one more alternative route for reaching James Bay *via* Albany, and one that has also been very carefully explored. This would make the north-east shore of Lake Nepigon its starting point.† Lake Nepigon, as will be observed by the map, lies nearly due north of Thunder Bay, communication between the two lakes being maintained by the Népigon River. The level of Nepigon is, however, some 250 feet above Superior, and, therefore, a lift of that extent would be required to improve the inter-navigation of the two lakes. That once provided, a clear stretch of one hundred miles would be secured and, if the

---

* Report Select Committee House of Commons 1749, p. 221.
† Geological Survey 1871-2, p. 101.

prospects of a large mineral production on the shores of Lake Nepigon be realised, as there seems good reason to believe they will, such a work would probably, in time, be demanded, by the exigencies of that and its dependent industries. From Lake Nepigon the Ombabika River is the first stream to be passed on the route to the Albany. The distance to the summit level of the height of land, where Shoal Lake discharges its waters, both north and south, is 25 miles. So easy is the passage of the height of land here that Mr. Bell in his report says: " No portage occurs on the Ombabika for about nine miles before reaching Shoal Lake nor for nearly five miles beyond its northern outlet, so that we passed the height of land with the greatest possible ease, having had about seventeen miles of uninterrupted canoe navigation from the time we made the last portage in going up on the southern side till we came to the first in going down on the northern." Shoal Lake has an elevation of scarcely 300 feet over Lake Nepigon. The distance given, 25 miles, is, by measurement, on direct line. The distance following the course of the stream would be 42 miles. If, however, a road were cut to the point at which the open navigation, mentioned by Mr. Bell, nine miles south of Shoal Lake, commences, it is probable it need not exceed some 18 to 20 miles in length the several portages on the Ombabika would be avoided and the rise of 300 feet easily overcome.

The Powitik River, which is the northern discharge of Shoal Lake, after a course of six miles joins the Ka-pi-ko-ton-gwa, which was descended by Mr. Bell and his party for twenty-one miles, where the Mokoké River was entered and the canoe route north-westward pursued to the Zhob-schquay, and by that stream the Ogoké, a branch of the Albany, was reached, a large river 500 feet in breadth and fifty to sixty feet deep with lagoons and marshes on either side. These features it is reported to maintain for a long distance both above and below the junction of the Zhob-schquay, although, still lower down, it spreads itself out to a great width and becomes very shallow. But, leaving the Ogoké, the party entered the French channel, and at the end of a couple of miles, striking across a height of land that separates the Ogoké from the Ka-ge-i-na-gami, another tributary of the Albany, finally arrived at its junction with the Albany at a lake known as Lake Abazotikitchewan, a distance in a straight line of 83 miles from the mouth of the Ombabika River, or 142 miles according to the measurement of the distances actually travelled. In the course of the journey there are thirty-three portages, or twenty-nine, if a bend of the Ombabika be avoided by making one portage of sixty-six chains in length, by which means a distance of eight miles of river navigation may also be saved. From Abazotikitchewan Lake to Makokebatan Lake the distance is eight miles, but although there are several rapids there are no portages, the width of the river extending from ten or twelve chains at the rapids, to a mile in the intervening spaces. Makokebatan Lake is a fine sheet of water, sixteen miles in length, by a mile and a half in width. The Albany leaves the last-named lake by two channels, which reunite at Moosewaké Lake, twenty miles below Makokebatan. The northern channel has, meantime, flowed through a lake called Washi-saigan, or Lake of the Narrows, formerly known as Gloucester Lake, from a Hudson's Bay post so called that once stood in the vicinity. From Moosewaké Lake to Martin's Falls, in a distance of twenty miles, the river is full of islands and rapids. Martin's Falls, so called, is really only a rapid of some 12 or 15 feet easy descent, and readily passed by canoes. Between Makoketaban Lake and Martin's Falls, there are fifteen portages. But, at the Falls, the character of the river changes. The Falls are full 120 miles above the junction of the Kenogami River with the Albany, which, as already stated, is probably 150 miles from James Bay. For the whole course of 250 to 270 miles to the sea, the Albany is from twenty to thirty chains in width, from five to twenty feet (averaging about eleven feet) deep, and has a mean velocity of three miles an hour. In the opinion of Mr. Bell, the river would, except in very low water, be navigable by powerful steamers of light draught all the way from its mouth to the Falls. At Martin's Falls is a Hudson's Bay Post, "where hay, turnips, and potatoes have, for a long time, been successfully cultivated, and cattle thrive well." The river is open, as shown by the journal kept at the post for six months in the year. So free is it from obstructions below the Falls, that the Hudson's Bay boats, in descending, are allowed to drift all night with the stream, the submerged top of a pine tree being sufficient to keep them in the channel.

The total distances traversed by the surveying party are given in the report as follows :—

	Miles.
From Lake Nepigon to the Albany	142
Albany to the mouth of the Kenogami River	184
Kenogami mouth to James Bay	150
Total Miles	476

or, from Thunder Bay one hundred miles more, making the entire distance 576 miles. The question of actual distance, however, is of even less importance than the facilities of this route as compared with others. It must be recollected that, at Thunder Bay, there is already a considerable population, and one of a very enterprising character; that it is the head of the great lake navigation, and also likely to be the resort of a very large tonnage of vessels from the United States as well as from Canada. In view of a trade being opened up either with any section of the region intervening, or with Hudson's Bay, the considerations suggested must have great weight. Again, the Hudson's Bay Company were, aforetime, accustomed to bring in their goods from Europe *via* Moose for distribution at Fort William and other stations, the payment of customs rates, in the absence of governmental supervision, being thus avoided. And if it should turn out that a trade with Europe can be opened from Hudson's Bay to any extent, the busy and growing communities on the shores of Lake Superior and beyond, would naturally expect to benefit by their comparative contiguity to an Atlantic port. We may find, too, in the course of our inquiries, that the mineral region around Nepigon, as well as Superior, will need supplies that a more fertile region to the northward will afford, and for which a route corresponding with some of those already traced out will have to be found. Dividing the course followed by Mr. Bell into open, and obstructed or interrupted sections we have the following result:—

From Nepigon by the Ombabika with the portages, to the Shoal Lake and Powitik River seventeen mile reach, 33 miles, reduced by 68 chains portage at bend to ...... 25 miles.
From seventeen mile reach (open)... .... 17 "
To Albany at Lake Abazotikitchewan (with portages) ..... 92 "
Lake Abazotikitchewan to Martin's Falls (with portages) 64 "
Martin's Falls to James' Bay (open)...................... 270 "

468 miles.

With one sweep of 270 miles, the distance in which any interruptions to an unimpeded traffic occur, is thus reduced to less than 200 miles between the great inland lakes and the ocean, and there does not appear to be anything in the nature of the country to make such local improvements as may be needed to facilitate travel or the carriage of freight unreasonably expensive. The explorations of Mr. Bell and his assistants, have been, it is evident, conducted with great intelligence and perseverance. Still they have been, of necessity, more or less hurried, and consequently partial. A very careful examination of the whole country would be needed before pronouncing authoritatively on the advantages of the respective routes, the prospects of settlement, the tokens of latent wealth, or the means of reducing the labour of a journey from point to point to a minimum.

LAKE ABBITIBBE ROUTE.

The reports of the Geological Survey do not contain any account of explorations over the River Abbitibbe to Moose Factory, although that route has, doubtless, been, in past times, well travelled by voyageurs coming by way of the Ottawa River, from the head waters of which it is separated by only a short distance. Lake Abbitibbe lies nearly east and west, a little north of the height of land and on the Ontario and Quebec Boundary line, about one-fourth of its area, according to the Government maps, being in the latter Province. The River Abbitibbe may be said to rise in the height of land and to flow through the Lake, for the same name is given to its most important feeder from the southward as that of the stream that issues from its western extremity and, after a dip to the south, flows northwest to James Bay. From Lac des Quinze—an expansion of the Ottawa described by Mr. McOuat of the Geological Survey* as in most parts about a mile wide and some twenty-three miles in length—with the exception of one short portage at a fall of four or five feet on Lonely River, the navigation for canoes is uninterrupted to within half a mile of the height of land which separates the waters of the Ottawa from the rivers flowing into Hudson's Bay, and there is scarcely a perceptible current to overcome. The distance is thirty-one miles. The height of land is but some three-quarters of a mile to a mile in length. That passed, the waters of the Abbitibbe are touched at a small lake lying at the foot of the height of land, Lake Abbitibbe itself being reached by way of Lake Matawagogig, eight miles and Lake Agotawekaim, six miles long, connected by a small stream with four short portages in a distance of eleven miles. Here the southern Abbitibbe is struck and traversed for nine miles until it joins the Lake. Adding together the several stretches of water and portage the distance to Lake Abbitibbe from Lac des Quinze will be about 67 miles, and from the height of land 35 miles. The total length of Lake Abbitibbe, or rather of the two lakes into which it is divided, is forty-seven miles. From the south-west corner flows the northern Abbitibbe, first south-west, then west, to its first fall, a distance of seven miles. From this point in a straight line to its mouth, where it enters James Bay by the same outlet as the Moose, the length is about 200 miles, making an approximate distance by this route, allowing for the sinuosities of the river, of probably 350 miles from the height of land or 380 from Lac des Quinze, to James Bay. Traces of iron are found in the neighbourhood of Lake Abbitibbe but not in large quantities, and one curious feature is a magnetic island situated about the middle of the west side of the lower lake, so powerfully attractive that the surveyors' compasses were useless in its vicinity. On the northern slope of the height of land "groves of white pine were observed in all directions" "several pine trees were measured and found to be eight or nine feet in circumference." White spruce, yellow birch and cedar, are also tolerably abundant and of good size, some good specimens of the latter being noticed in the hollows among the hills on the south shore of Lake Abbitibbe. Around the lake itself pine is scarce, although a few well-grown trees were noticed. "Lake Abbitibbe," says Mr. McOuat, "is surrounded on all sides by level clay land; *** several acres are cultivated at the Hudson's Bay Post, and a French Canadian, who has been more than thirty years at Abbitibbe, although the only crop now raised there is potatoes, insisted that all the ordinary cereals could be cultivated as successfully at Abbitibbe as on the St. Lawrence.

FROM LAKE NEPIGON TO LAKE ST. JOSEPH.

In following up the explorations of Mr. Bell, we have incidentally surveyed the larger portion of the tract forming the eastern half of North-Western Ontario. The only section remaining is that lying between Lake Nepigon and Lake St

---

* Geological Survey, 1872-3, p. 119 et seq.

Joseph or the head waters of the Albany. This region, like all the rest of the new territory, is intersected with rivers, lakes, and streams. The construction of the Canadian Pacific Railway will do much towards utilizing these means of access to the more remote districts. The information at command leads to the opinion that it is neither a desert nor altogether inhospitable. At Lake Wabigon the Indians cultivate maize, and although in a country so prolific of pine as is Canada other woods are in danger of being undervalued as an element of national wealth the spruce and tamarac, which seem to become finer and more valuable the further, north they extend, are a class of timber that bear a good merchantable reputation, where they can be easily and cheaply conveyed to market. The tamarac for railway purposes finds an enormous consumption, which will increase as the construction of lines either by the Government or as the result of private enterprise is promoted in the North-west, while for ship-building, it is an excellent material.

Physical Peculiarities and Aspect of Eastern Division.

Occasional reference has been already made to the physical peculiarities and aspects of the country traversed by the surveyors of the routes to Hudson's Bay from Lakes Nepigon, Superior and Huron. A little closer examination of the information at command on this point, may be interesting. The termination of the portages and the comparative smoothness with which the rivers falling into James Bay pursue their course from points at a considerable distance from their ultimate destination is thus accounted for:* "Between the great lakes and James Bay, the country is of a very different character in each of the two geological areas which it embraces, namely, the Laurentian and Huronian plateau, and the palæozoic and (probably) tertiary basin of James Bay. The former is somewhat elevated, undulating, and dotted with great numbers of lakes, while the latter is low, level, and swampy, and as far as known generally free from lakes, constituting a well-marked geographical as well as geological basin, bounded by a distinct vein of hard, ancient rocks for five-sixths of its circumference, since it contracts to a width of only about 200 miles, where it opens into Hudson's Bay on a line between Capes Jones (on the east), and Henrietta Maria (on the west). This rim is high, and has a steep slope towards the centre all round. Owing to the unyielding nature of the rocks, all the rivers running into James Bay meet with a great and generally very rapid descent on reaching the edge of this basin. As a consequence, the "long portages" on all of them occur where they pour down this slope." While the term rocky is very generally applied to the whole of the area lying between the lakes and James Bay, it is asserted, on very good authority, that the proportion that is "rocky" in the popular signification of the term, is less than is commonly supposed. Mr. Bell, who, from his continuous and

---

* Geological Survey, 1875-6, p. 338.

very able devotion to the study of the subject, we are again tempted to cite, points out that the fact of the high and rocky points being more conspicuous than the levels, and the further fact that the portages usually occur at rocky places, is very likely to produce a generally exaggerated and erroneous impression.* He goes on to remark: "Loose materials of some kind actually cover the greater proportion of the area, and in a very considerable per centage of it, the soil is more or less suited for agriculture. Its precise nature, in various sections, has been, described in my reports from 1869 to the present one. As a matter of experience in this sort of country, in the district of Algoma and elsewhere, the quantity of cultivable land, on the establishment of settlements, always proves to be much greater than it appeared while in a state of nature. In a general way there is perhaps a greater proportion of good soil in the plateau region northward than southward of the height of land." This will apply, probably, with great fairness, not only to the area referred to as a whole, but to the most limited portions that may be traced along the courses and on either branch of the rivers. The general aspect of the country traversed by the Mattagami or south branch of the Moose, is undulating, but the inequalities do "not often exceed one or two hundred feet." Rock crops up here and there, the land otherwise consisting of a a sandy and gravelly subsoil, underlaid by bouldery earth or clay, and having more or less vegetable loam upon the surface. From the foot of the Long Portage to the sea, the basin already described is entered. The banks of the river are not often high, and are usually composed of gravelly and bouldery earth and clay. The banks sustain a second growth of poplar, and white birch, with some coniferous trees, but at a short distance back, the ground is swampy and covered with black spruce and tamaracs growing on a deep layer of sphagnum moss. The islands and mainland about the mouth of the river, consist of alluvial earth well suited for cultivation. Farming and gardening have been very successfully carried on at the Hudson's Bay posts at Lakes Mattagami and Missinibi. At Missinibi spring wheat has been grown and turned out well. The climate becomes more moderate as the slope towards James Bay is descended, the lower level being a compensation for the increasing latitude. The red and white pine are both found in the neighbourhoods of Mattagami and Kenogamissee Lakes, and also at Lake Missinibi, but not further north. Indications of mineral deposits present themselves at various points on the route, and large deposits of gypsum occur on the Moose, near James Bay. A specimen of lignite from the main Moose River gave the following analysis:†

	Slow coking.	Fast coking.
Fixed Carbon	45.82	44.03
Voluble combustible matter	39.60	41.39

---

* Geological Survey, 1875-6, p. 339.
† Geological Survey, 1875-6. p. 422.

	Slow coking.	Fast coking.
Water	11.74	11.74
Ash	2.84	2.84
	100.00	100.00
Ratio of voluble to fixed combustible	1.16	1.06

The lignite is very similar to some found in the Souris Valley, and also to specimens collected for analysis from the neighbourhood of Dirt Hills and Woody Mountain in the North-west Territory. An analysis of ore from a large deposit on the Moose, at the foot of the Grand Rapid and below the Long Portage, has yielded 52.42 per cent. of metallic iron.*

JAMES BAY.

Having noticed most of the several approaches to James Bay from the south and west, and supplied at all events material on which some calculations may be made as to its accessibility, we shall direct our attention to the Bay itself and its more immediate neighbourhood. James Bay is a sheet of water 300 miles in length, measured from its most southerly point, to a line drawn from Cape Jones, on its eastern, to Cape Henrietta Maria, on its western coast, where it suddenly expands, and Hudson's Bay is entered, of which James Bay is simply an inlet. James Bay, except at its southern end, where it becomes irregular and more narrow, is about 150 miles in width, its shores being almost parallel for nearly 250 miles. It received its name from Captain James, one of the Northwest passage explorers, who wintered in the Bay at Charlton Island, in the year 1631. It is described as being so shallow that, with the exception of a channel down its centre, the bottom may be touched with an oar by a person rowing in a small boat when almost out of sight of shore. The ship channel runs from a point opposite Moose Factory, in the south of the Bay the whole distance to Mansfield Island in Hudson's Bay, 750 miles north in nearly a straight line. In traversing this channel a chain of islands, 500 miles long, is passed, many of them of large size, and having rivers that discharge into the larger or smaller Bay. The southern and western shores of the Bay, which represent the portion forming the Ontario Boundary, are low and level, and owing to the extreme shallowness of the water at some places, they are difficult of approach from the Bay. "Between high tide water mark and the woods," says Mr. Bell,† " there is generally a broad space or marshy belt interspersed with willow bushes and divided by muddy creeks. In some places this open border is raised above all but the highest spring tides, and constitutes a level prairie, supporting a rich growth of grasses and sedges. The marshy outline of the shore of the Bay is often interrupted by points and peninsula-

---

* Geological Survey, 1875-6. p. 431.
† Geological Survey, 1875-6, p. 322.

like islands composed of boulders piled together in thousands, with scarcely any fine material among them." In the southern part of James' Bay the water, although tidal and brackish, is in some parts so free from saline matter as to be used for drinking. This peculiarity is ascribed to the immense volume of fresh water poured into the bay from the great rivers of which it is the outlet. Its muddiness, caused by the ebb and flow of the tides over so shallow a bottom, is also fatal to the existence of fish, which, conseqently have to be sought for in a more northerly situation.

Moose Factory.

Moose Factory, at the mouth of the river of that name, is situated on a small island, six or seven miles from the Bay. The factories of the Hudson's Bay Company are not located anywhere with a view to the advantages of settlement, convenience for trade with the Indians and hunters, and protection in more troublous times than the present, having been the objects most in view in the selection of their sites. The soil at Moose Factory is of cold wet clay, on a level and quite undrained. Nevertheless, oats, barley, beans, peas, turnips, beets, carrots, cabbages, onions, and tomatoes, are grown with no more care for their protection or production than is shown in any other part of Canada. A crop of 1,700 bushels of potatoes was harvested in 1874, and wheat, accidentally sown, had ripened although no experiments as to the ordinary capacity of the soil and climate for its production on a larger scale appear to have been recently made. That this is no barren or famine-stricken land may also be seen from the fact that, at Moose Factory there is quite an establishment of horses, sheep, and pigs, in addition to eighty head of cattle. The Right Reverend Dr. Anderson,[*] in his evidence before the House of Commons Committee, in 1857, suggested that the means of living were more precarious than formerly at Moose Factory, but his remark probably applied to wild geese or other resources of the Indians, and not to those of settlers depending on the cultivation of the soil or domestic live stock. Mr. George Gladman, who was literally a child of the Hudson's Bay Company, for he was born at New Brunswick, one of their posts on the Moose River, and resided at Moose Factory fifteen years, gave a very favourable account of the productions of the district.[†] He stated that the climate and soil were good; that potatoes and vegetables were raised in great abundance; that barley ripened well; that small fruits, such as currants, gooseberries, strawberries and raspberries were plentiful and grew wild; that wheat, owing to the shortness of the season, had never been tried, but that horned cattle, horses, sheep and pigs, were kept there and did well. They required, of course, to be housed in the winter. At Albany, which lies in latitude 52 degrees 8 minutes, north, the climate and soil, Mr. Gladman stated, were similar to those at Moose Fort, although it is considerably further north. It is well sheltered and the

---

[*] Report Select Committee on Hudson's Bay Co. to the House of Commons (Eng.), 1857, p. 241.
[†] Report Select Committee on Hudson's Bay Co. to the House of Commons (Eng.), 1857, p. 391.

marshes on the banks of the river and shores of the Bay yield inexhaustible supplies of hay, a fact that is worthy of notice in connection with settlement in any part of the James Bay area, as securing an abundant and cheap fodder for cattle.

Sir George Simpson, on the other hand, discouraged the idea that the soil could be successfully or profitably cultivated at Moose Fort.* "Barley," he said, "very seldom ripens, the potatoes are exceedingly small, and the crops unproductive." But Sir George Simpson was too clearly convicted, during his examination of partisan feeling in favour of the Hudson's Bay Company, and too antagonistic, to the opening-up of their close preserve, to be accepted as a reliable witness in opposition to the independent testimony of other persons. Nor are we confined to the assertions of those whose reports have been already quoted, although no good reason exists for casting doubts upon them. The capacity of the James Bay region for supporting any population that the temptations of commerce may draw thither, and that is, practically, all we need to know, were perfectly well understood a hundred and fifty years since. In a description of the countries adjoining Hudson's Bay, published in 1744,† is a statement by a Mr. Frost, who had resided at Moose Factory since 1730, and who gave a very good account of the climate and country there, and of the river southward. The purport of Mr. Frost's information was, that on the banks of the Moose wild rice grew in great abundance, the Indians beating it off the plant into their canoes when ripe, and that all sorts of grain could be raised in the vicinity of the river a little to the southward, while, at Moose Factory, barley, peas, and beans, thrive well, "although exposed to the chilling winds which come from the ice on the Bay." In the woods at the bottom of the bay, he goes on to say, both at Moose and Albany, as well as at Rupert's River (on the east coast), are large trees of oak ash, pine, cedar and spruce. "They have," he adds, "exceeding good grass which improves every day as they cut and feed it, and may have everywhere within land all sorts of pulse and grain, and all sorts of fruit trees as in the same climate in Europe; for what sorts they have tried throve well." In another book published in 1752,‡ it is stated that at Moose Factory " sown wheat has stood the winter frosts and grown very well the summer following, and that black cherries also have grown and borne fruit. Before the Commons' Committee in 1749, several witnesses gave evidence confirmatory of the above.§ Mr. Edward Thompson, three years surgeon at Moose Factory, had seen far better barley and oats grow at Moose River than he ever saw in the Orkneys; but the quantity sown was small. The seed would bear sowing again, but diminished in goodness. "There was ground enough broke for this corn (grain), but never any encouragement given for sowing it. but quite the reverse, the Governor forbidding it for no other

---

* Report Select Committee on Hudson's Bay Co. to House of Commons (Eng.), 1857, p. 46.

† An account of the countries adjoining Hudson's Bay, by Arthur Hobbs, Esq., London, 1744, p. 45.

‡ An account of six years' residence in Hudson's Bay, by Joseph Robson, London, 1752.

§ Report of Select Committee on the State of the Hudson's Bay Company, 1749, p. 222.

reason, than that *if corn (grain) had been sown, a colony would soon have been erected there."* The residents of any settlements on the shores of James Bay would not, however, be confined to food raised by agricultural labour. The rivers abound in pike, trout. perch and a fish, probably white fish, from the description. Enormous flocks of wild geese frequent the rivers and bay, and countless flights of wild duck breed in the marshes near the mouths of the Moose and Albany. As many as 20,000 wild geese have been shot in one season, the slaughter only being stayed because no more were needed. In addition to these, there is an abundance of partridges, plovers and other birds familiar to the sportsman.

Climate at Moose and Albany.

Mr. Bell, as previously mentioned, gives the neighbourhood of the Bay credit for a milder climate than is experienced further inland at a higher level. Mr. Frost, quoted in Hobbs' work, states that, at Moose Factory the ice breaks up in April. Mr. Matthew Sergeant, an employé of the Hudson Bay Company, in his evidence before the Committee in 1749, stated, that the thaw begins at Albany about the 8th or 10th of April, when there is a good soil for six or eight inches which may be gained within a fortnight after the beginning of the thaw; that in two or three weeks more it thaws to the depth of two feet, commonly by the beginning of May; and the frost sets in again about the beginning of October; but the frosts break sooner up in the country and come in later.* A journal kept at Albany Factory gives an exact account of the weather and climate at that post in the years 1729-31.† The frost, it is recorded in this document, began in October in 1729, about which time the geese that had returned from the northward to that River in August, departed from thence to the more southern countries. The creek near the Factory was frozen over on the 13th; by the 21st there was a good deal of ice floating in the river; by the 31st it was fast as far as Charles Creek; by the 5th November the whole river was frozen over, but not so strong as to bear; the weather was temperate with some snow to the 27th; all the month of December was interchangeably three or four days cold, and then a temperate frost with some snow; the month of January much the same, cold and temperate interchangeably; the month of February was variable but mostly moderate, at intervals warm, and then sharp weather; March to the 8th was warm, temperate frost; from that time to the 17th fine clear weather, with some snow; thence to 29th clear weather, tolerably warm; on the 30th a storm of snow; and then it began to thaw in the middle of the day; it continued thawing till the 5th of April, then two days frost; it thawed again till the 13th after the geese returned from the southward; then to 17th raw, cold weather; 18th warm and rain; then interchangeably warm and raw weather until the 28th, when the frost

---

* Report, 1749, p. 220.
† Hobbs, p. 12.

was broken up in the country by the freshes (freshets) coming down; the 29th the ice gave way to the head of the island, and next day drove down to Baily's Island, when all the marshes were overflowed, the Bay not being yet thawed; the ice continued driving in the river until the 5th of May, then the river fell five feet by the breaking up of the ice at sea; the 7th they had thunder and rain, the ice still driving in the river; the 8th the Indians came down in their canoes to trade; to 13th they had raw, cold weather; 16th they began to dig their garden; 22nd the tide began to flow regularly; the 23rd they sowed their turnips; the geese then went to the southward to breed; raw, cold weather until the 29th; 30th variable weather with some hail and snow; from that time till the 12th of July fine warm weather; then to the 7th September warm or very hot weather; to the 18th warm and temperate; then to the 25th variable and temperate with some rain; then frost in the night; fine weather until the 29th; October 2nd and 3rd some frost and snow in the night; to the 12th fine weather; stopped fishing, having no frost to freeze the fish; to the 24th fine warm weather with small frost; the 28th ice in the river and the geese going away; November 13th the river full of heavy ice; the 18th it was moderate weather; the winter was not so severe as the former; the geese returned the 14th of April, 1731; the freshets came down May 5th, the 12th the ice was gone to sea; the 13th the Indians came down to trade in their canoes; they had fine warm weather that year from the 11th of May to the middle of September. The Albany was frozen over on the 10th of November. This perfectly reliable narrative certainly does not show the climate of James Bay to be more severe than in many of the settled portions of Canada. That 1729 was not exceptionally mild, is evident from the remark, that, in 1730, it was not so severe as in the former year. There is nothing in the description here given to show that the inhabitants of the south shore of James Bay need want for any of the ordinary pleasures or comforts of life, or be more unfavourably circumstanced in regard to the length of the inclement season, than many of their fellow countrymen even in some other portions of the Province of Ontario. The attractions to settlement will be only ascertained after more thorough and systematic explorations than were possible in the brief period of time allotted to the surveyors of the Geological Department, and, although the officers of the Hudson's Bay Company have now thrown off the reserve once enjoined upon them, and show much praiseworthy anxiety to afford information as to the resources of the country, there has never been, under their auspices, any such thorough and exhaustive examination of its hidden treasures as the indications of their existence would justify.

MINERAL RESOURCES OF JAMES BAY AND NEIGHBOURHOOD.

While at Moose Factory in 1875, Mr. Bell was presented with specimens of massive iron pyrites, dark, smoky chert, like that of Thunder Bay, epidosite, agate, carnelian, quarry crystals, galena, and black crystalline siderite, containing rather a large amount of manganese, all from the mouth of Little Whale River. Little Whale River is on the east coast of Hudson's Bay near the northern extremity of James Bay, and north-east of Moose Factory. It is consequently not within the limits of the Province of Ontario, but its accessibility from Moose River renders its deposits available to any enterprise directed from that point. Mr. Bell, in his report says :* "The conglomerates are said to be largely developed between Cape Jones and Little Whale River. At Moose Factory, I was shown a pile of flagstones which had been brought from an island about seven miles north of Little Whale River. This rock is a very fine-grained semi-crystalline non-calcareous olive-grey felsite. I was given some chips of a somewhat similar, but slightly calcareous rock, holding bunches of small crystals of iron pyrites, which were said to have came from the same vicinity." The specimens of lignite found on the Moose River or rather at the mouth of Coal Brook, a confluent of the Moose, and analysed by Mr. Hoffman, have been already referred to. Another object of interest, and one demanding careful research, is the appearance of a mineral that closely resembles, if it is not the true, anthracite. Mr. Hoffman's report of his analysis of a specimen of anthracite from Whale River is as follows :†

"It is not improbable that the mineral may have an origin analogous to that of the black anthracite matter which occurs in many places in the Quebec group, as also in the chert beds among the upper copper-bearing rocks of Lake Superior, and alluded to in the Geology of Canada, 1863, pages 525 and 68. The specimen examined was very compact, homogeneous; colour, pitch black; powder, deep black; lustre, bright metallic; fracture, highly conchoidal; it does not soil the fingers. When boiled in a solution of caustic potash, it was apparently unacted on; the solution remained colourless, and the powder black. Gradually heated, or when projected into a bright, red-hot crucible, in either case decrepitated but very slightly." The following is the mean of two very closely concordant analyses:—

Fixed carbon	94.91.
Volatile combustible matter	1.29.
Water	3.45.
Ash	0.35.
	100.00.

Coal, whether anthracite or bituminous, is so potent a factor in all commercial operations, whether as a mechanical agent or as an article of traffic, that the most important results might flow from the discovery of any extensive deposits within

---

* Geological Survey, 1875-6, p. 323.
† Geological Survey, 1875-6, p. 423.

a distance not more remote from the commercial centres of Ontario than many of their present sources of supply. Mr. Hoffman* also reports that a specimen of iron ore from a large deposit on the north-west side of the south branch of the Moose River, at the foot of Grand Rapid, below the Long Portage, contained 52.42 per cent. of metallic iron. Mr. Bell, speaking of this ore, says :† "The position of the deposit is on the north-west side of the river, at the foot of the rapids. It runs along the cliff for a distance of upwards of 300 yards, with an exposed breadth of twenty to twenty-five yards. The highest points rise about fifteen feet above the level of the river. The surface is mottled, reddish-yellow and brown, and has a rough, spongy, or 'lumpy' appearance, like that of a great mass of bog ore. On the surface, and sometimes to a depth of several inches, it is a compact, brown hematite, occasionally in botryoidal crusts, with a radiating columnar structure; but deeper down it is a dark-grey, compact, very finely crystalline spathic ore, apparently of a pure quality. The brown hematite evidently results from the conversion of the carbonate. The former yields, according to the analysis of Mr. Hoffman, 52.42 per cent. of metallic iron, while the latter shows a very small amount of insoluble matter; indeed there is, chemically, little room for impurities, since it gives rise to so rich a brown hematite."

The gypsum beds on the Moose are thus described :‡ "The bank on the south-east side runs for above two miles; that on the opposite side about half that distance. The gypsum consists of a bed of the ordinary hydrous saccharoidal variety running along each side of the river and rising to a height of not more than ten feet above low-water mark. It is mostly of a light-bluish grey colour, with some whitish portions coloured or mottled with yellow and other colours. The white variety, suitable for making stucco, was not observed to be in sufficient quantity to be of economic value. * * * * A gypsum bank, similar to the last, runs along the south-east side of the river, between four and five miles below the extremity of the higher one, on the same side."

In a letter which recently appeared in the Toronto *Globe*, Mr. William Hickson, a gentleman of evident intelligence and powers of observation, and formerly in the employ of the Hudson's Bay Company, thus refers to the mineral deposits on the shores of James Bay: "At a certain point on the east coast of James Bay there is a vein of magnetic iron, so extensive, that, when examined by a practical English miner in 1865, it was pronounced by that gentleman to be one of the most valuable veins of that ore in existence. Plumbago, in a pure state, is also to be found in the same locality; and at this place is the commencement, on the sea coast, of a range of mineral-bearing rocks, which extend along the main land, and among the islands near the shore, for a distance of 600 miles, with a

---

* Geological Survey, 1875-6, p. 431.
† Geological Survey, 1875-6, p. 321.
‡ Geological Survey, 1875-6, p. 321.

width of from fifty to two hundred miles or more, into the interior of the country. * ¯* * * At certain points on this range a partial examination has been made, showing that galena, iron, and copper are procurable in almost unlimited quantities, and during a thirteen years' residence at various parts on this east coast, I had ample opportunities for examining both its geological and mineralogical formations, at a great many points, both in James and Hudson's Bay, and have no hesitation in stating that I believe it to be the most valuable mineral region in the Dominion, perhaps on this continent."

THE WILD ANIMALS OF NORTH-WESTERN ONTARIO.

Most of the wild animals of North-Western Ontario are to be found in greater or less numbers over both the eastern and western portions. Cariboo range all through the territory, either singly or in small parties of eight or ten. A curious change in the habits of these creatures has been noticed, and one that certainly speaks wonders for their instinct, if the circumstances be as related. It was formerly the habit of the cariboo to migrate during winter in vast herds to the colder regions north of the Nelson River. Thousands of them collected together for their northern march, the crossing of the Nelson being always effected at pretty nearly the same period every year. This fact being well known, they were watched for, and a certain number were killed, their condition in the fall being very favourable for the purposes of the hunter. But, in one fatal year (1832), a grand *battue* was arranged; Indians and whites gathered from all parts for one tremendous massacre. The poor cariboo were slaughtered by wholesale, and in sheer sport, the carcases that could not be consumed or carried off floating in heaps down the waters of the Nelson to Hudson's Bay. And—strange to tell—the cariboo have, since that terrible day in the annals of cariboo history, never crossed the Nelson again. The Moose are becoming very scarce in the region west and north of Lake Superior, although still plentiful, it is said, in the neighbourhood of Lake Nipissing. Black bears are very numerous everywhere. In the vicinity of James Bay and Hudson's Bay, there is a bear, dark-brown in colour, and in form halfway between the common black and polar bear. This bear is exceedingly fierce and dangerous to attack, while the black bear is seldom known to show ferocity of disposition. The latter may be tamed, but the brown bear of Hudson's Bay is untameable and resists, even when captured young, all attempts at its domestication. Wolves are scarce, as also are their chief prey, the red deer. Red deer once abounded in the region west of Lake Superior, but the destruction of the forests by a great fire about 200 years ago, or near the time of the advent of the first white settlers— and the signs of which are seen in the age of vast forests of trees of about 200 years' growth—drove out or destroyed the red deer, deprived them of their means of support, and, probably, led to the migration of the wolves to places where they too would secure food and shelter. Buffalo were seen by early settlers near Rainy River, but they are not now found nearer than some 300 miles west of Fort

Garry. The lynx is frequently met with, and so too is the thievish and mischievous wolverine.

The rabbit, or rather hare—for it is of the character of the latter animal the Canadian representative of the genus partakes—is ubiquitous here as elsewhere. The rabbit is the chief food of most of the smaller carnivora and their numbers largely depend on his fecundity. In times past too, the Indians found in the rabbit their staff of life. His flesh was their meat, his skin, worked up into every form of robe and garment, was their chief covering. But there came trouble to rabbits and to their human, as well as brute, destroyers. In 1868 a pestilence attacked the rabbits of the whole northern part of the continent. They died in millions, and, in Quebec, local authority had to be invoked to prevent the diseased bodies of rabbits picked-up in the woods being sold in the markets. The Indians, who had most depended on rabbits for their supply of food, were terribly distressed and but for the progress of the Dawson road, and works connected therewith, many would have starved. As it was, some 200 were engaged by Mr. Dawson and thus temporarily supported. It is to be mentioned to their honour, that they showed the utmost anxiety to send to their suffering families all they could earn and spare from their own necessities. The rabbits are now again multiplying as only rabbits do multiply. There is a sort of tradition that they are cut off, or fail to increase, periodically about once in seven years, but this is probably only a local belief. It is not a small allowance of rabbit, however, that will satisfy the needs of a hungry man, white or Indian. The flesh contains but a small proportion of nourishment, and three or four rabbits per diem are not too many for an ordinary backwoods or pioneer appetite. The common brown, and the more rare and very beautiful silver fox, are among the denizens of North Western Ontario. The black fox, a beautiful creature with silky hair, and whose skin sells for as much as forty pounds sterling, while an ordinary fox skin is not worth more than a dollar, is now and then seen and captured, but, as the price paid for his coat would imply, is regarded as a very extraordinary spoil by the hunter.

Beaver abound on the streams and creeks. It is satisfactory to learn, too, that they are increasing instead of diminishing. In the early days of settlement the Indians and white trappers took pains to preserve the beaver from extinction. But, with the invention of beaver hats and other demands upon the beaver's coat, the price of beaver skins rose, and cupidity got the better of prudence. For some years, however, furs have been low in price and the use of beaver for hats has all but ceased, so the beaver is recuperating his numerical strength. The otter, fisher, and mink, are plentiful; while, in the more northern regions, the marten attains a high degree of beauty and corresponding value. The musk-rat builds whole cities of his dwellings on the banks of the rivers and seems to defy the destructive operations of his enemies, for he flourishes and even increases, although, in the Rainy River District alone, no less than 90,000 musk-rat skins have been collected in a single year. The beaver and musk-rat are both "good eating" and figure prominently in the Indian dietary. The ermine, a very beautiful and easily tamed creature, is also a familiar acquaintance of the Indian and settler. The ermine is of a brown colour in summer, but in winter becomes perfectly white, with a black tip on its tail, in which condition it is most valuable for marketable purposes. The opossum is a native of the territory and in the southern part the porcupine is occasionally found. His flesh is a delicacy. The common red-squirrel abounds and there are a great many large squirrels both of a brown and grey colour. An unpretending but very prolific creature is the deer-mouse, looking, as it poises itself on its hind legs, like a diminutive kangaroo. It is of a hybernating disposition and, like the squirrel, provides an ample winter store, a colony of deer-mice having been known to carry off half a barrel of peas that had been left unprotected. Of the odorous skunk and every other American representative of the weasel tribe there are varieties enough to gratify the most passionate student of that branch of natural history. Many of the feathered inhabitants of the territory have been referred to already. The partridge, fantail grouse and water fowl of all kinds, are extremely plentiful. The feathers of the wild goose and the down of the wild swan have long been articles of trade by the Hudson's Bay Company.

Indians of James Bay.

The Indians of James Bay and western shore of Hudson's Bay are like those of the Rainy River district, members of the great Algonquin family. A large area of country, lying between Nelson River on the north and Lake Superior, has not yet been the subject of treaty arrangements with its aboriginal possessors. The Indians subsist largely by the chase, and the sale of its produce to the Hudson's Bay Company. At Moose River Post, York Factory, and on the English River, the Church Missionary Society has maintained stations, ahd, according to the testimony of the Right Rev. Dr. Anderson, already mentioned in connection with the Parliamentary Committee in London in 1857, the results have been satisfactory.* The Bishop, as previously noticed, took an unfavourable view of the agricultural capabilities of the country and, according to his evidence, some such views must have more or less affected the policy he directed. The difficulty of producing permanently serious impressions on men leading a purely roving life, or inducing them to conform to habits of settled industry, is almost insuperable. But, in addition to the direct benefits, in a religious sense, conferred by missionary efforts, the influence on the relations of the two races exercised by the presence of such an organization as that of the society referred to can be but advantageous in elevating the tone of a population in its primitive state, and giving the Indians a sense of having in their midst disinterested advisers or protectors.

---

* Report of Committee, p. 236.

Dr. Andersons's motives for objecting to the abolition of the Hudson's Bay Company's monopoly in furs were indicated in a memorial he addressed to the Governor and Committee of the Company, in which he says:* "After four years' residence in Canada, my opinions are unchanged as to the evils that would follow free trade in furs. It would doubtless enable unscrupulous adventurers to make money in the southern part of the territory. Rum would be largely used, and the Indians greatly demoralized, and difficulties thrown in the way of missionary operations. I never hesitate to express my opinion to that effect, whenever I am asked what I think of the movement." The admirable effects of the policy pursued by the Government of Canada towards the Indians of the North-west Territories, and the general result of the system, on which the whole Indian population of the Dominion is provided for, have dispelled many of the fears others besides Dr. Anderson may have once entertained as to an influx of white settlers. But it is easy to see how, looking at the questions before him from such a point of view, he may, unconsciously perhaps, have done an injustice even to the character of the country itself.

Hudson's Bay.

Our references have hitherto been mainly to matters directly bearing upon the interests of the Province of Ontario in the territory now brought within its jurisdiction. But, in the waters and country lying beyond the boundary line fixed by the arbitrators, the people of Ontario have, in common with the whole Dominion, also an interest, and, from their geographical position, it may be anticipated that they have even a larger stake in the explorations and developments of those regions than others. To them, if communications be established with James Bay, the whole coast line of Hudson's Bay will be accessible, as also will the fisheries in its waters, while, should it be attempted to utilize the Nelson River Valley as a route for the transportation of the products of the Saskatchewan Valley to Europe, settlements would of necessity spring up on the Nelson or Hayes Rivers, and their confluents, and probably on the western shores of the Bay also; if, too, the expectations that the eastern coasts contain large mineral deposits be realized, a demand for the products of Ontario manufactures would naturally present itself in that quarter also. It is true that, as we shall presently see, some eminently respectable authorities are sanguine, that the navigation of the Bay and Straits may be effected for a period in the course of the year, sufficient to make it profitable, and to justify very bold measures for connecting the Saskatchewan and Lake Winnipeg, with Hudson's Bay by means more expeditious than those now existing. The progress of modern science has done so much to remove old prejudices and to overcome presumed impossibilities that it would be wrong hastily to decide adversely to these views. But certainly the evidence so far before

---

* Report of Committee, p. 238.

us does not go to prove, by any means, that the bulk of the cereal products of the West could be forwarded to York Factory in time to admit of their being shipped to Liverpool during the open season. That this might be done on a small scale and for, perhaps, several successive years, is likely, but it is only by attracting shipping in the ordinary course of commerce, and that, too, in considerable numbers, that a trade, suited to the exigencies of those engaged in it, can be carried on. The advent of an early winter and the consequent detention or dismissal without freights, of a fleet of merchant vessels, would be ruinous in its effects, and, in all probability discourage such ventures for many a year to come. On the other hand, if, in the Hudson's Bay region, there are substantial foundations for local enterprise, it may find a safe and uninterrupted outlet by way of the Canadian lakes or St. Lawrence, to either the American or European market; and meantime the possibility of using the mouth of the Nelson River as an ocean port may be experimentally tested for a series of years with the certainty that, if the experiment be successful commerce will not be long in securing whatever advantages it has to offer.

THE NELSON VALLEY ROUTE.

Although the Nelson River has been the highway of traffic and used as the means of communication between Hudson's Bay and the interior for well nigh two hundred years, it is to day as little known to the people of this continent generally or of Great Britain as was, till recently, the great river the travels of Henry M. Stanley have rendered so famous. But, with the growth of a new power in British North America, and the rapid progress of colonization in the North-west, it is all but certain that the Nelson will ere long become as familiar to Canadians, at all events, as is to-day the Red River or the Assiniboine. When it is recollected that, while Lake Winnipeg is 2500 miles from the seaboard of the Gulf of St. Lawrence, and lies exactly in the centre of the American continent, under the 57th parallel, its northern extremity is only 380 miles from the tide waters of Hudson's Bay, the inducements to bring the interests of the North-west into closer relations with this comparatively contiguous ocean port are very great indeed. The Nelson and Hayes Rivers both flow from the westward, and, after a considerable divergence of route, enter Hudson's Bay nearly together. It is at the mouth of the Hayes River that York Factory, the chief trading post of the Company on Hudson's Bay, is situated, in latitude 57 deg. 10 m. north. It is about 650 miles in a direct line north-west from Moose Factory overland; by sea, 750 miles. Prince of Wales Fort, at the mouth of the Churchill, is 150 miles further to the north-west. The Nelson is the only outlet of the waters of the Lake Winnipeg Basin, including the North and South Saskatchewan. Its fall, in its whole course of nearly 380 miles, is trifling, not exceeding twenty inches to the mile. While, therefore, the voyager proceeding eastward with his produce has the benefit of a "down grade," his return trip is not so laborious as in the case of many of the river highways of commerce. The Nelson River proper is less frequented than the Hayes and the chain of rivers with which it is connected. The reason assigned by the Hudson's Bay Company for preferring the Hayes for their batteaux is, that there exists danger in "tracking" in the Nelson, from the large blocks of ice hanging from its precipitous banks. The Indians, too, choose the Hayes, because of the accessibility of the Factory at its mouth, which, in their light canoes, it would at times be difficult to reach from the Nelson. The following is the route, with distances marked, as furnished by the surveyor of the Hudson's Bay Company and referred to by Professor Hind, in his evidence given before the Immigration and Colonisation Committee at Ottawa last session:*

	Miles.
York Factory	0
Hayes River	52
Steel River	27
Hill River to first fall	32
Fall to upper part of river	30
Lac de la Savanne	7
Jack River (Riviere aux Brochets)	10
Knee Lake	47
Front River	13
Holy Lake	30
Small brooks and lakes on a great plateau	50
Brook with Beaver Dam (Each-away Man's Brook)	28
Hare Lake	7
Sea River (part of the Nelson)	35
Play Green Lake (Norway House)	14
Total Geographical miles	382

In the year 1846 a body of troops, under the command of Lieut.-Col. Crofton, were sent by the York Factory and Lake Winnipeg route, to Fort Garry, a distance of 700 miles. The troops consisted of a wing of the 6th Foot, a detachment of artillery and a detachment of Royal Engineers. The force numbered 383 persons, including 18 officers, 329 men, 17 women, and 19 children. With its equipment and four guns, it occupied thirty days in the trip, but the commander reached his destination in twenty-three days from York Factory. The journey was accomplished without accident, or, apparently, any difficulty, except those incidental to portaging. Lieut.-Col. Crofton, in his evidence before the Commons

---

* Report of Committee, p. 155.

Committee in 1857, produced a list of the portages made by him on the line of route. They are thirty-four in number, as below: *

Name of Portage.	Length in Paces.	Nature of Ground.
Rock Portage	48	Hard, dry, even.
Borrowicks	39	Rocky, swampy.
White Mud	43	Swampy.
Point of Rocks	61	Hard, rugged.
Brassa	482	Hard and uneven.
Lower Burntwood	476	Dry and even.
Morgans	266	Rocky, broken.
Upper Burntwood	59	Dry, rather uneven.
Rocky Ledge	63	Hard, rugged.
Mossy	503	Swampy and slippery.
Smoothrock	347	Hard, even.
First Portage	42	Swampy.
Second Portage	58	Swampy.
Devils' Portage	173	Hard. Difficult landing.
Ground Water Creek	51	Swampy.
Lower Creek	62	Swampy.
Long Water Creek	521	Swampy.
Second Water Creek	68	Swampy.
Upper Water Creek	53	Swampy.
Front Fall	49	Rocky, even.
Creek Fall	31	Rocky, swampy.
Knife Portage	59	Swampy.
Upper Portage	40	Swampy.
Lower Portage	38	Swampy.
Moore's	56	Swampy.
Crooked Spout	36	Rocky, swampy.
Upper Spout	42	Swampy.
Hill Portage	243	Rocky, rugged.
Upper Portage	57	Rocky, rugged.
Whitefall, Robinson's	1,760	Level, but slippery.
Painted Stone	16	Rocky, even.
First Dam	28	Hard, stony.
Second Dam	25	Hard, stony.
Sea River	63	Rocky, even.

The journey from Norway House to Fort Garry would, of course, be accomplished without obstruction by way of Lake Winnipeg and the Red River.

CLIMATE.

In the Valley of the Nelson there is considerable cultivable land, nor is the climate one of extraordinary severity. That the seasons become milder and the winters shorter as the westerly course is taken is proved by many incidents on record. In Ellis' Voyage† it is mentioned that the ice in Hayes River, where his ships had wintered, gave way on the 16th of May, and, on the 5th of June, nineteen canoes, laden with furs, passed the vessels on their way to York Factory, a clear proof that the rivers westward had been open at least a fortnight or three

---
* Report of Committee, p. 181.
† Voyage to Hudson's Bay, 1746-7.

weeks previously. Hearne relates, that in 1775,* he and his companions killed teal in the rivers they passed through from Cumberland House to York Fort, as late as the 20th October. This shows, not only that the birds in question defer their emigration until the end of October, but that navigation is also open up to, or past that date. In his evidence before the Immigration and Colonization Committee, Professor Hind stated as follows: †"The warm and moisture-laden winds from the Pacific moving north-easterly, deposit much of their moisture on the western flanks of the Rocky Mountains. Rising over the summit of the ranges, they are deflected to the south by the combined influence of the earth's rotation and the pressure of the compensating cold winds from the north. The cold winds acquire their maximum influence on the 95th meridian, which passes through the Lake of the Woods. Farther to the eastward, the isothermals are pressed back by the warm winds from the Gulf of Mexico, which push them to the north-eastward. In both cases the rotation of the earth is a leading cause in determining the course of the fertile zones. These, be it observed, are broad generalizations, subject to numerous local modifications, which affect local climates. The Valley of the Nelson appears to exhibit one of these local modifications, arising from its low level above the sea. Until within thirty miles of Port Nelson the canoe route down Hayes River shows little difference in point of climate from the canoe route of Lake Superior, where it crosses the height of land. The cause, however, in this case is, in part, assignable to the difference in elevation above the sea level, which is upwards of eleven hundred feet; this would theoretically produce a difference in temperature equal to more than three degrees of Fahrenheit. All accounts agree in stating that the climate of the valley of the Nelson River changes greatly as soon as a distance of some five and twenty or thirty miles from the sea is reached. The cold winds from Hudson's Bay lower the temperature in the vicinity of the sea-board to a great extent, but, thirty miles inland, their influence is greatly modified."

Joseph La France, in his narrative,‡ states that "within four or five leagues of the sea at York Fort the cold continued, and there was ice in the river in June, when, above that, they had a fine spring, all the trees in bloom, and very warm weather up to the Great Fork, in the beginning of June." According to Ballantyne,§ vegetation in the valley of Hayes River, thirty miles from its mouth, on the 23rd of June was found to be in an advanced state, the trees being covered with foliage and, on the 25th of June, he describes the spring to have long begun on Hill River, and "along its gently sloping banks the country was teeming with vegetable and animal life." This is on the canoe route from York Factory to Norway House and a little to the south of the valley

---

* Journey to the Northern Ocean.
† Report of Committee, 1878, p. 153.
‡ Appendix to House of Commons (Eng.) Committee, 1749.
§ Ballantyne's Hudson Bay.

of Nelson River proper. Oxford House is situated on Holy Lake, and Lieut. Chappel remarks,* that owing to the richness of the soil, and the geniality of the climate, this place produces a number of excellent vegetables. Dr. King who was attached to Captain Back's journey to the Arctic Ocean,† states that at the commencement of Hill River, halfway between York Factory and Norway House, the argillaceous cliffs are seen rising in some places 100 feet above the water level, capped with hills of at least twice that height; and at some parts of the stream, where it is expanded to a breadth of several miles, innumerable islands appear, stretching in long vistas, and well-wooded, producing scenery of extreme beauty. The occurrence of such deep deposits of drift clay in this valley is of great importance. The same traveller states, that Steel River—the name which Hill River takes after flowing fifty-seven miles—serpentines through a well-wooded valley, presenting at every turn much beautiful scenery, but nothing to equal what is seen along the shores of the former stream. The mouth of Steel River is forty-eight miles from the sea by the winding course of Hayes River into which it falls. Professor Hind, in the course of his evidence, remarked: ‡ "The brigade of the Hudson's Bay Company's boats for the interior, usually leaves York Factory about the end of May, which shows that the rivers are open even in the cold border land within twenty miles of Hudson's Bay. We must bear in mind that ice is often found in the Lakes near the water-shed, west of Lake Superior, about the middle of May, and Lake Winnipeg is sometimes impassable at its northern extremity during the first week of June. From these comparisons, it will be seen that the climate of the Nelson River valley is of an exceptionally favourable character away from the coast line. It can scarcely excite surprise that there should be a large tract with a good climate, and great depth of drift clays in the vicinity of the valley of the Nelson River, for it is the lowest portion of the whole basin of Lake Winnipeg, and is constantly under the influence of the drainage waters from three hundred thousand square miles of land, lying altogether to the south of the narrow depression, not, perhaps, more than forty miles broad, through which the Nelson River finds its way. The great thickness of drift clays upon several of the rivers, noticed by different observers, on the canoe route from York Factory to Norway House, must necessarily produce a good soil, and the two conditions of a good soil and a humid climate concur to sustain an exceptionally fine forest growth for this region, and an abundance of animal life." With the information we have at command respecting the Nelson River valley, we may safely come to the conclusion, that, if not a region to which large numbers of persons are likely to resort exclusively by reason of special attractions for the agriculturist, it is one that would furnish abundant supplies for communities settled on

---

* Narrative of a voyage to Hudson's Bay, 1817.
† Narrative of a journey to the shores of the Arctic Ocean 1833-4-5, by Richard King, M. R. C. S.
‡ Report of I. & C. Committee, Appendix to Journals, Canada, 1878, p. 154.

SOIL AND CLIMATE AT YORK AND CHURCHILL.

the shores of Hudson's Bay, or for any shipping that might resort to its western ports.

With the fact just referred to in view, the precise conditions of soil and climate at York Factory, or the mouth of the Churchill, are of secondary importance. On this point the statements are a little contradictory. Dr. Rae, in his evidence before the Commons Committee in 1857, was asked* "how the climate at York Factory compared with that of the Orkneys." His answer was to the effect, that the character of the summers was about the same in both cases, but that the winters were longer, extending over seven or eight months, beginning in November and not actually ending before June. Sir George Simpson also spoke † unfavourably of the productiveness of the soil around York, owing to the presence of ice in the ground for most of the year. Mr. A. Isbister, ‡ on the other hand, pointed out that frost in the subsoil does not necessarily prevent the growth of vegetation, if the thaw extends to a reasonable depth. In Siberia, he remarked, which is in the same latitude as the northern part of the Hudson's Bay territories, there are large crops of wheat every year. With the process of clearing the country the sun's rays would penetrate deeper and the thaw be more complete. The testimony of Sir John Richardson § and Mr. George Gladman was rather unfavourable than otherwise to the cultivable capacity of the soil at York Factory. Mr. Joseph Robson, six years resident in Hudson's Bay, already referred to, while admitting the presence of frost at from three to four feet depth in the ground, alleged that the surface of the ground was free from ice from the latter end of May to the end of August; that he had suffered more from cold in England than at York Factory, the clothing at the latter place being adapted to the climate; and that the soil bore roots such as carrots, radishes and turnips, as well as many other kinds of vegetables. In his opinion, if the land was properly cultivated it would support numbers of people. The want of proper cultivation, including drainage, has, no doubt, a good deal to do with the rather, on the whole, unfavourable picture given of the agricultural or horticultural capabilities of the neighbourhood around York Factory.

Robson, who appears to have been a very intelligent persons, says:¶ "The soil about York Fort is much better than at Churchill. Most kinds of garden stuff grow here to perfection, particularly peas and beans. I have seen a small pea growing without any culture; and am of opinion that barley would flourish here. Gooseberries and black currants are found in the woods, growing upon such bushes as in England. Up the river, are patches of very good

---

* Report Hudson's Bay Committee, 1857, p. 31.
† Report of Committee of Hudson's Bay Company, 1857, p. 46.
‡ Hudson's Bay Committee, 1857, p. 136.
§ Hudson's Bay Committee, 1857.
¶ Six years' residence, p. 43.

ground; and battones under banks so defended from the north and north-west winds, that there is a fine thaw below when the top is freezing; here, whole families might procure a comfortable subsistence, if they were as industrious as they are in their own country. Upon Hayes river, fifteen miles from the fort, is such a bank as I have just mentioned, near which I pitched my tent. After paling in some ground for a coney-warren, and for oxen, sheep, goats, &c., I should expect by no more labour than would be proper for my health, to procure a desirable livelihood; not at all doubting of my being able to raise peas and beans, barley and, probably, other kinds of grain. The island on which York Factory stands is more capable of improvement than can be imagined in such a latitude, and so near the Bay. It is narrow, twenty miles up from the Bay, so that drains might be cut to very useful purpose. I cut a drain near the Fort, to dry a piece of ground for a battery of four cannon which afterwards wore quite a new face; the snow did not lie upon it so long as before and grain flourished with new vigour. I observed also, that, before the snow was thoroughly thawed, several vegetables were springing up beneath it; and by the time it had left only a very thin shell of ice, these vegetables were grown up three or four inches." Some other experiments by Mr. Robson confirmed his opinion that, with draining, a good soil for garden cultivation could be obtained and a considerable quantity of produce raised. As professor Hind reminded the Committee at Ottawa last session,* in all these northern latitudes the duration of light as well as the intensity of the sun's rays must be taken into account as a compensating influence in relation to vegetable growth. He submitted to the Committee the following table giving the relative intensity of the sun and the length of day in latitudes 40°, 50° and 60° respectively, and therefore embracing the whole area of territory referred to in this paper.†

TABLE Showing the Sun's Relative Intensity, and the Length of the Day in Latitudes 40°, 50° and 60°.

	Latitude 40°.		Latitude 50°.		Latitude 60°.	
	Sun's Intensity.	Length of Day.	Sun's Intensity.	Length of Day.	Sun's Intensity.	Length of Day.
		H. M.		H. M.		H. M.
May 1	80	13.46	77	14.30	70	15.44
do 16	85	14.16	83	15.16	79	16.56
do 31	88	14.38	87	15.50	85	17.56
June 15	90	14.50	89	16.08	88	18.28
July 1	90	14.46	89	16.04	88	18.18
do 16	87	14.34	86	15.42	84	17.42
do 31	84	14.08	81	15.04	77	16.38
Aug. 15	79	13.36	74	14.18	68	15.24
do 30	72	13.02	65	13.28	57	14.08
Sept. 14	65	12.22	58	12.32	46	12.46
do 29	57	11.44	47	11.36	36	11.26

* Report of I. & C. Committee, p. 152.
† Report of I. & C. Committee, p. 153.

Commenting on this table the Professor says: "It will be seen that in latitude 40° the sun's intensity is represented by 88 on May 31st, the day being 14 hours 38 minutes long. In latitude 50° the sun's relative intensity of light and heat on the same day is 87, but the day is 15 hours and 50 minutes long. In latitude 60° which is some degrees north of Peace River, (and nearly three degrees north of York Factory) the sun's intensity on the 31st of May is represented by 85, but the day is 17 hours 56 minutes long. During the fortnight from June 15th to July 1st the sun's intensity closely approximates in latitudes 40°, 50° and 60°; but the day is widely different in length, and the heat and light have a greater time to act on vegetation under the more northern meridians. Thus from June 15th to July 1st the sun's intensity diminishes from 90 to 88 between latitude 40° and latitude 60°; the day, however, on July 1st is 14 hours 46 minutes long in lat. 40°; 16 hours 4 minutes long in latitude 50°; and 18 hours 18 minutes long in latitude 60°."

The Hudson's Bay Post at the mouth of the Churchill River, 59° is subject substantially to the conditions of light, heat and length of day, described in the last column of the foregoing table. It is spoken of by old travellers as being more favourably situated than the other factories for trade, in consequence of its greater distance from the French (in Canada), who interfered greatly with the operations of the incorporated monopolists of the fur trade. The Churchill is described by Hobbs as "a noble river, navigable for 150 leagues, and, after passing the Falls navigable to far distant countries." Its sources are near the height of land in long. 110° W., whence by a very devious route it winds its way east and north-east to Hudson's Bay, at one point approaching very near to the confluents of the Nelson, and the waters of Lake Winnipeg. The climate at the Fort is not by any means intolerable. Captain Middleton wintered there with his ship in 1741. His diary,* shows that snow fell first on the 1st of September, after which the weather was unsettled, the river being frozen over so as to admit of crossing upon the ice, on the 9th of October. On the 1st of June the ice gave way in the channel and drove down to sea, but was still fast on the flats. Partridges in large numbers were killed during the whole winter, wolves, foxes and other animals also being seen near the Fort. At Churchill, as well as at York and the more southern posts, the wild goose is one of the most regular sources of subsistence, thousands of these birds being killed and preserved for winter food. All kinds of wild fowl abound in these latitudes to quite as great an extent as at Moose or Albany. There is a good supply of wood in the vicinity of Churchill, and, as at other points, any quantity of hay growing in the marshes, and furnishing food for cattle. Seal River lies still further to the northward than Churchill, and, according to Hobbs, the musk-ox is or was in his time met with between the two rivers.

---

* Hobbs, p. 14.

NAVIGATION OF HUDSON'S BAY.

In regard to the navigation of Hudson's Bay, Mr. Walter Dickson, the correspondent of the Toronto *Globe*, previously mentioned, expresses himself in the following terms:—"This inland sea of Hudson's Bay—which might well be termed the Mediterranean of Canada—is upwards of twelve hundred miles in length (including, of course, James Bay) with a width varying from ninety to three (five) hundred miles and upwards, with several hundreds of islands studded over its surface, some of them of such extent as to have large lakes and rivers on them, giving altogether a sea-board of upwards of two thousand miles (more than that of the United Kingdom of Great Britain), and so easy of access that an ordinary screw steamer might start from Quebec and reach any point on its coast in considerably less than two weeks. That so little information concerning this great inland sea of the Dominion has been given to the world, is simply owing to the fact, that, for upwards of two centuries, this sea and the land surrounding were virtually the property of the great monopoly the Hudson's Bay Company, who made it their study, as it was to their interest to keep Hudson's Bay, like all the rest of the territory over which they held sway, as completely unknown to the outer world as possible * * * * The sea of Hudson's Bay itself is so little known that there are no charts of it in existence excepting those made by the Hudson's Bay Company, and they are only useful as guides to the depots at certain points on the east and west coasts of the Bay."

Professor Hind states * that "the most recent Admiralty map of Hudson's Straits exhibits a want of full information regarding the coast lines on both sides of the Straits." A chart published in 1853 and corrected up to 1872 retains errors perceivable in those constructed in Queen Elizabeth's reign. The practical tests of the navigation of the Bay have been confined to slow sailing merchant ships sometimes convoyed by men-of-war, not less worthy the appellation of tubs, as compared with the vessels of the present time, sent out on any service supposed to require special qualifications in the direction of speed, strength and security. Yet, it is alleged, that, since their original occupation of the coasts of the Bay two centuries ago only two of the Hudson's Bay Companys own ships have been lost, and that through culpable recklessness. It is quite probable, however, that the navigation of Hudson's Bay will soon be robbed of some of its terrors, and that what has been regarded as hazardous or impossible will be found, by the aid of the new and powerful agencies modern discovery has provided, both safe and practicable. The contrast in other respects between the experience of twenty years since and that of to-day is rather amusingly exemplified by a perusal of the evidence of Captain Herd one of the witnesses before the committee of 1857.† "I do not think," said the worthy captain,

---

* Report I. and C. Committee, 1878, p. 136.
† Report Hudson's Bay Committee, 1857, p. 256.

"that a steamer would do at all among ice, to force a passage. * * * If I were asked my experience I would prefer a sailing ship among ice to a steamer." He would have been loth to believe that, in a very few years, the whole conditions of the great sealing industry would be changed by the adoption of steamers in place of sailing vessels, and that the hardy seal hunters, so far from avoiding, would actually seek the very ice that he was wont to encounter in his sailing ship, and enter it as fearlessly as he steered his craft in open water. With stout screw steamers, protected as are these used in the Newfoundland seal fisheries, and furnished with the magneto-electric light, there is very little loose ice that need preclude a passage where an end is to be gained by attempting it.

Hudson's Straits.

Hudson's Straits, the only outlet of the Bay, are at its north-eastern extremity. They are about 500 miles in length and vary in width from 45 miles at the entrance between Resolution Island on the north and Britton Islands on the south shore to three times that extent in other places. The Strait, like the Bay, contains numerous islands affording excellent shelter and harbourage. The Hudson's Bay ships, according to a table compiled by Lieut. Chappell, R. N. in 1814* had usually arrived abreast of Charles Island on the south side and near the western entrance of the Straits, at periods varying from the last week in July to the beginning of September. Captain Herd, before the Committee in 1857, stated that he usually arrived at York Factory about the 10th or 15th of August, and left again from the 15th to the 25th of September.† The time occupied in going through the Straits on the westward trip in July and returning in August or September in sailing vessels, differs greatly, varying from three weeks to a month in the former case and from three to five days in the latter, the Straits in August or September being free of ice. Professor Hind's theory ‡ is that Hudson's Straits are never frozen over and that the ice brought down in July is not even from Hudson's Bay but from a more northerly region, whence it reaches Hudson's Straits through Fox Channel. The heavy tides in the Straits are strongly against the notion of solid ice being formed there. There is very good authority for believing that the ice formed in Hudson's Bay, does not leave the Bay at all, but that its dissolution takes place in the Bay itself. In the southern parts of Hudson's Bay and in James Bay nearly the whole surface may be frozen over. But the water there is shallow, and, in James Bay, from causes already stated, contains very little salt. On the contrary, in the upper portions of Hudson's Bay the main body of the water, it is believed, does not freeze at all. Hearne, referring to a fact in ornithology, mentioned by Pennant,§ alludes quite

---

* Narrative of a voyage to Hudson's Bay, 1817.
† Report Hudson's Bay Committee, 1857, p. 255.
‡ Report of I. and C. Committee, 1878.
§ Journey to the Northern Ocean, p. 429.

incidentally to the ice being frozen "several miles from the shore," the implication being that the ice was limited in its extent to a distance from the shore which the term "several miles" would be popularly supposed to represent. Another fact, too, confirmatory of the belief that Hudson's Bay is not the source of the ice-pack that crushes through Hudson's Straits, is, that, after passing Charles Island, near the western entrance of the Straits, ice is seldom seen, except it is met with floating in the centre of the Bay. The proposition, however, that the passage of the Straits cannot be safely made before the middle of July has been very generally endorsed by navigators of great experience, including Sir Edward Parry. But the view held to-day by Professor Hind and other more recent authorities, namely, that an entrance could be effected and the Bay reached in June, is not a new one.

Robson, in his book already frequently referred to,* and which was published in 1752, advocated the passage being attempted in June. He says: "At York Fort and Churchill River I have observed that the ice did not break off close at the shore, but gradually; the first field leaving the shore-ice two or three miles broad, the second less, and so on until it was cleared away. These several fields of ice drive through the Straits; but as they go off at intervals, one field may be driven through before the next enters from the Bay; consequently the Strait is sometimes pretty clear of ice. As the Straits, then, *are never frozen over*, nor always unnavigable, even when there is much ice in the Bay, I imagine that a safe passage may often be made about the beginning of June; for, as the ice enters the Straits at intervals, according as it breaks off, and as the wind and currents drive it out of the Bay, so the wind may keep the ice back at this season, as at any other. Besides, the ice at the bottom (southern end) of the Bay, and the north and west ice, will not have had time to reach the Straits, but after June all the Bay ice commonly reaches it. The beginning of June, therefore, seems to be the likeliest time in which to expect a free passage." Robson's idea as to the ice being from the Bay was probably incorrect, but his information as to the ice-movements in the Straits may nevertheless have been perfectly sound. Lieutenant Chappell, R. N.,† was also of opinion that the Straits might be entered in June. The danger, if any exists, would be rather in the entrance of the Straits than in their subsequent navigation. The ice at the mouth of the Straits is exposed to all the force of the Atlantic, but, once in the Straits, a vessel, if warned by signals of danger, could easily take refuge in one of the numerous places of shelter on the coast or one of the Islands in the Straits. Professor Hind‡ suggests the establishment of signal stations, from which mariners could be advised as to the drift of the ice as affected by the winds, and thus usually secure a more or less open channel. In fact, if the iron-protected screw steamer, thus aided and guided, did not al-

---

* Six Years' Residence in Hudson's Bay, p. 58.
† Narrative of a Voyage to Hudson's Bay.
‡ Report of Immigration and Colonization Committee, 1878.

ways succeed in overcoming the obstructions arising from this flow-ice in the Straits, the difficulties it presents would be reduced to their smallest proportions. It is understood that Professor Hind's theory has the full endorsation of Professor Bell, whose next issued report of his most recent explorations will be looked for with great interest.

Hudson's Bay Fisheries, Minerals, and Commerce.

Calculations as to permanent trade and intercourse cannot, of course, be based on exceptional experiences. It is, however, a fact attested by recent visitors to the coasts of Hudson's Bay and James Bay, that for the past two seasons there has been little or no ice in either, while Hudson's Straits have also been very clear, and navigation quite unimpeded. To what this state of things may be attributable it is difficult to say, and how long it may continue, is of course quite uncertain. But it is interesting as affording one more proof that Hudson's Bay is not the ice-bound sea it was once endeavoured to make the world believe.

The accessibility or otherwise of Hudson's Bay and Straits for several months in the year, will have an important influence on the development of its fisheries, which have yet received but little attention. Ungarva Bay, just within the eastern entrance of Hudson's Straits, has already an excellent reputation as the field of an extensive seal and whale fishery. In an interesting little *brochure* recently issued by Lieut.-Colonel Dennis, Deputy-Minister of the Interior,[*] a table is given from American official sources, showing the returns of American whaling vessels fishing in Hudson's Bay from the year 1861 to 1876. The favourite resort of these vessels is Marble Island, in the north-east part of Hudson's Bay. Their numbers varied from one to fifteen in a season, the total number in the fifteen years being forty-nine. Another return of the value of the catch for the eleven years—1861 to 1874, omitting 1869 and 1871—was $1,371,023. Seals and porpoises, among the larger denizens of the ocean, are also to be found in the waters of the Bay or Straits. On the north-western shore of the bay is a very prolific salmon fishery, capable, apparently, of forming a most important local industry. Although there is no evidence published of cod being captured alive, their remains have been frequently found on the shore, and the resort to the Bay of enormous shoals of caplin—the chief food of the cod—is regarded as one of the best proofs that the cod are not far behind them.

With the fur-trade, which still finds, at the mouths of the great rivers that fall into Hudson's Bay, its principal depots; with the mineral wealth that will inevitably, at no distant day, be extracted from the coasts of these hitherto almost unexplored waters; from the fisheries that may be stimulated as the facili-

---

[*] Navigation of Hudson's Bay. Ottawa, 1878.

ties for navigation become better understood, and from the fertile soil on the banks of the great western rivers, may accrue results most important to the people of Canada, and in these it is desirable that the Province of Ontario, looking, as it does, to this vast northern sea as one of its boundaries, should as early as possible participate. The question of establishing improved communications between the more populous sections of Ontario and its north-western territory, especially with the settlements on Lake Superior, will undoubtedly ere long engage fuller attention. The practicability of constructing a railway to Sault Ste. Marie from the most advanced point of existing railway communications, has long since been demonstrated. The late Mr. Herrick, and other surveyors, have furnished information pointing to the comparative ease by which connections in winter, by means of a stage road, might be maintained with Thunder Bay, the inhabitants of which region are now practically isolated for six months in the year. Lake Superior, on the other hand, never freezes over, nor is it a stormy water, and even Thunder Bay is open till so late a period that, with vessels properly protected in the bows it would be possible to maintain traffic, via the Sault, for nine months out of the twelve. The Sault certainly appears to be the point to which railway enterprise will have to be directed as providing a way to intercourse with North-western Ontario and the vast territories lying both to the north and west of the boundaries of this Province.

ERRATA.

On page 2, line 18, for " south " of the said river read " source " of the said river.
On page 3, fourth line from foot, for Rainy " River " read Rainy " Lake."
On page 7, under head " Inducements to Settlement," second line, for " southern " read " western."
On page 27, first line, for " York " read " Nelson," and on sixth line, for " western " read " eastern."
On page 40, fourteenth line from top, for " most " read " more."
On page 63, sixteenth line from foot, for " north-east " read " north-west."

ties for navigation become better understood, and from the fertile soil on the banks of the great western rivers, may accrue results most important to the people of Canada, and in these it is desirable that the Province of Ontario, looking, as it does, to this vast northern sea as one of its boundaries, should as early as possible participate. The question of establishing improved communications between the more populous sections of Ontario and its north-western territory, especially with the settlements on Lake Superior, will undoubtedly ere long engage fuller attention. The practicability of constructing a railway to Sault Ste. Marie from the most advanced point of existing railway communications, has long since been demonstrated. The late Mr. Herrick, and other surveyors, have furnished information

www.ingramcontent.com/pod-product-compliance
Lightning Source LLC
Chambersburg PA
CBHW020249090426

42735CB00010B/1865